Of Caves and Caving

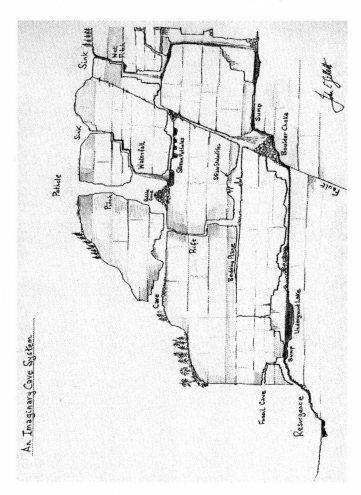

A Typical Cave System

Of Caves and Caving

◆

A Way and a Life

Text and sketches by John E Gillett

Writers Club Press

San Jose New York Lincoln Shanghai

Of Caves and Caving
A Way and a Life

Writers Club Press
an imprint of iUniverse, Inc.

For information address:
iUniverse, Inc.
5220 S. 16th St., Suite 200
Lincoln, NE 68512
www.iuniverse.com

Illustrations are by the Author

ISBN: 0-595-22057-6

Printed in the United States of America

Sine speluncis, vita est mortis imago.
—David Heap

Contents

Foreword

Throughout my caving career that spans more than forty years I have been frequently asked the question, "Why do you go caving?" I have never been able to provide a satisfactory answer, but this book comes tantalisingly close to explaining the reasons why apparently sane, rational individuals are driven by some mysterious force to take seemingly senseless risks in the pursuit of pleasure. John's exciting journey takes us through a series of adventures beginning at a time when potholers were regarded as rather eccentric, a belief reinforced by the popular press, hungry for news of every mishap or accident.

The journey continues as an eloquently written whistle-stop tour spanning four decades and several continents giving an insight, as perhaps only John can, into "what makes cavers tick." There is something here for everyone—from the experienced hard man to non-caver alike, with tales to suit all tastes, of exploits from the humorous to terrifying, with interesting anecdotes that will maintain the readers' interest throughout. Each step of the journey keeps one wondering what lies around the next corner. At the end of the adventure we are brought right up to date with a visit to a system only recently discovered after more than twelve years of excavation revealed what is "one of the best stream-ways in Britain."

Ralph Johnson: *January 2002*

Acknowledgements

My sincere thanks to all of my friends, family and caving companions whose names are in this book. Without their help, hospitality, strength and companionship my caving life would have been empty.

John Gillett

Chronology

18-May-58 Dow Cave

02-Aug-59 Aggy

10-Dec-59 Sump 1

20-Aug-60 Popova Polje

28-Mar-70 Saint Catherine's to Fisherstreet

13-Jun-76 Water Icicle

16-Aug-79 Oyanbelza

17-May-80 Birks Fell

26-Jun-80 Swinsto

12-Jul-80 Gaping Ghyll

09-Aug-80 Pilgrimage to Pierre Saint Martin

02-May-81 OFD1-2

24-Oct-81 Helictite Heaven

05-Aug-83 The Hall of the Thirteen

08-Aug-84 "Allumez le feu"

01-Sep-84 3000ft up 3000ft down

13-Aug-86 Canyon de Sadum

05-Apr-87 Les Manants

21-Jul-87 Cueto Coventosa

30-Jul-88 Molle Pierre

05-Jul-89 Stari Hrad

06-Oct-91 El Buxu

15-Oct-95 Sterkfontein

03-Feb-02 Notts 2

Introduction

This book is written for you. You may have chosen it by chance or received it as a present. Alternatively, you may have chosen it on purpose. In either case, it is in your hand, so let your curiosity guide you to read further inside its covers.

We may not know each other and when you read this I may be long gone, but this book connects us momentarily like a handshake. Welcome to the view of an ordinary caver's world.

Our perception of the world around us may differ, but in the underlying process we are both playing our small part. Mine is to interest you and maybe to change your opinions about caving. I hope that you enjoy the articles and anecdotes that follow. They are intended to give a taste of caves and caving. Not only of the caves themselves, but also of the cavers in their caving world—a world that changed considerably over the forty years and more that the author spent in it.

The book is written in chronological order, but may be dipped into at random. By reading from cover to cover, it should be possible to trace the changes in caving equipment and techniques over the last few decades. It may also be possible to trace the changes in the caving society, too. Read on.

J E Gillett

1

Dow Cave

I was raised in an era before television was freely available. As a result, I became an avid reader. The local library ticket allowed me to wander freely in worlds much wider and more varied than those afforded by modern television. Twothirds of my reading material was fiction, the rest nonfiction with a strong bias to the great outdoors. I particularly enjoyed mountaineering books and, whilst searching the shelves for new editions, stumbled on *One Thousand Metres Down,* a book by Jean Cadoux about the exploration of the Gouffre Berger. At that time, the Gouffre Berger was the deepest cave in the world. The descriptions of the explorers' adventures underground stimulated my imagination in the same way as Jules Verne's *Journey to the Centre of the Earth* which I had read in my childhood. So, when I met a real caver during my National Service, I had plenty of questions to ask him.

Boyd was a keen crosscountry runner and mountaineer as well as a dedicated caver. He was one of the founder members of the caving section of the Catterick "Dales Club" and acted as their meets secretary. We first met whilst skiing in Norway and there was ample time in the evenings for him to answer all of my questions. Boyd was a patient and enthusiastic caving mentor. It was not difficult for him to persuade me to take part in a caving trip when we returned to England.

A few weeks later, the time arrived for my first adventure underground. Boyd helped me to prepare for this on the Thursday beforehand. He provided me with an old miner's helmet made of papiermâché, a brass device that he said was a miner's lamp, a small Primus stove and some army combat rations. He advised me to pack these in a rucksack together with a sleeping bag, mess-tins, mug, cutlery, a set of army 'Long-johns', denim overalls and two pairs of socks. He also advised me to wear a comfortable pair of boots, as we would have to hike several miles to reach the cave. I later added a few other useful items such as an army tin opener, matches, boiled sweets, soap and a towel. He told me to rendezvous at Catterick Camp Centre bus stop very early on the following Saturday morning.

When I arrived, Boyd was already there with two other cavers. Boyd introduced me to his companions. They were both National Service-men and members of the "Dales Club." Doug was another keen fell-runner. Sandy was a six-foot tall geologist armed with a specimen hammer. Their rucksacks looked heavier than mine and I wondered what I had forgotten. We caught the bus to the neighbouring Yorkshire town of Richmond. As we travelled, Boyd explained that our intention was to reach the village of Kettlewell before evening, spend the night there and then go caving on Sunday before returning to Catterick.

We soon arrived at Richmond and after a short wait, caught the bus to West Burton in Wensleydale. This second bus-ride was longer and as we chatted, I learnt that we would have to travel about twelve miles on foot from West Burton to reach Kettlewell. Luckily my army training had prepared me for this and it was a relief to know that we did not have to carry weapons as well as our rucksacks. I vaguely understood that we would descend 'Dale' cave before retracing our route back to Richmond. I did not know the Yorkshire Dales at all and relied on Boyd's knowledge and expertise to get me there and back. (*A week later I realised that I had misheard the name of the cave and that we had visited Dow Cave. This just goes to show what an absolute beginner I was!*) As for the night, I learned that a friendly farmer in Kettlewell village had promised us beds in a straw barn attached to his farm.

The bus eventually arrived at the Wensleydale village of West Burton and stopped near the centre. We alighted, hitched our packs to our shoulders and strode off purposefully through the village and into the nearby Walden Dale. The five-mile walk up to Walden Head was most enjoyable. The narrow Dales lane revealed pleasant views along its length and we had the occasional company of a small beck to one side. At the end of the lane we struck uphill over rough ground leading up to the moors. Boyd took a compass bearing from the lane end and we were soon stumbling along over the heatherclad moorland. In spite of regular army exercises over similar ground, I began to feel the strain on my legs and soon began to breathe heavily. The three cavers were much fitter than I was, but I managed to keep up with them. An hour later, I was glad when they decided to take a rest at an old shooting hut. The thought crossed my mind that if this was the walk in, then what on earth was the cave going to be like?

After a brief snack, we continued on for about another mile across the heather to join a small road. This provided easier going and quickly led downhill to the twisting descent of Park Rash, a steep hill once used for motorcar trials. The afternoon sun sank lower in the sky as we continued our march along the road towards Kettlewell, but it was not long before we were on the final steep gradient down into the village.

At the farm, we received a warm welcome and were shown to a straw filled barn that was up a flight of stone steps over the byre. We grounded our packs, took out our Primus stoves, and before long we had mess tins of beans and mince steaming away and a brew of tea on the go. Fortified after our meal, we walked down to the village centre, light of foot without our heavy packs, to visit one of the local pubs. The pay of a National Serviceman was sufficient for a pint or two, but we did not overimbibe. Nightfall drew us back to the comfort of the barn and our sleeping bags on the straw. We could smell the warm breath of the cows below before sinking into oblivion.

We woke early to bright sunshine, took a quick wash in the farm kitchen and cooked porridge for breakfast. Without delay, we then repacked our rucksacks, said goodbye to the farmer and his wife, then made an early start for the cave. We had to keep a close watch on the time, as the last bus back from West Burton was our deadline. We had to allow enough time for the return walk over the moors after the caving trip.

The walk up the valley from Kettlewell did not take long and soon we were at the bottom of Park Rash again. Here we climbed over a wall to alight on a small footpath. The path to Dow Cave was truly scenic, contouring along the side of a steep-sided valley with a stream below. The path soon led us down to a small meadow of short grass dotted with orchids, heartsease and rare wild flowers. On the other side of the meadow we came to a small bridge at a junction of two streams. From here the route petered out to a narrow rocky ledge high above the stream that ended in a final scramble down to a slippery ford. Crossing the stream with care not to slip, we climbed up a steep path on the far side to a ruckle of large boulders. Lurking behind the rubble heap was the imposing gloomy entrance to Dow Cave. A slight mist of water vapour floated up into the sunlight that beamed through the trees. My first natural cave…Its earthy scents and cool breath touched my subconscious and I felt a prickle of excitement.

The others started to change into caving clothes, generating clouds of dust as they shook loose the mud from their last trip. We took off our surface clothes and put on our caving gear. Next to our skin, we wore army 'Long-johns,' issued to us three sizes too large and shrunk to size by the camp laundry. Over these, we wore old army denims and boots, topped with papier-mâché helmets that carried carbide lamps borrowed from the 'Dales Club.' My denims were spotlessly clean in comparison with the others' although my helmet looked just as mud-streaked and battered as theirs. Our clean walking clothes were placed in our rucksacks and hidden in the rocks for our return. Now for the lighting…

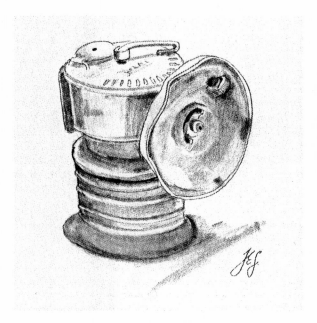

An old Carbide Lamp

We each had a small acetylene lamp for lighting our way underground. Boyd produced a long battered tin from his rucksack. He prized off the lid to reveal the calcium carbide lumps that would power our lamps. I was instructed to unscrew the lamp base, taking care not to lose the rubber washer from around its rim, and to fill it twothirds full of calcium carbide. The lumps were mostly metallic in appearance, some with a slight sparkle, and some covered with a yellow-white powder. When I dropped a small lump on the damp rock underfoot, it fizzed and fumed until I picked it up. It felt quite warm to the touch. I replaced the lamp base and screwed it up tightly to make a good seal on the rubber. Copying the others, I knelt down by the stream and sucked in a mouthful of water. Then, opening a small cap in the top of the lamp, I squirted the water from my mouth into its reservoir. One large mouthful was sufficient to fill this.

On the top of the reservoir was a thin lever that activated a small valve between the water reservoir and the carbide in the base of the lamp. This lever controlled the water flow to generate acetylene gas and could be positioned at various settings notched into the top of the reservoir. Now that the reservoir was full, I opened the valve to start the reaction.

The gas was supposed to emerge from a small jet at right angles to the reservoir in the centre of a round, shining reflector. I placed my tongue in front of the jet to feel if any gas was coming out. Nothing! I opened the valve a bit more. Still nothing! I shook the lamp. With a tremendous squirt, a column of water shot out of a small hole in the water reservoir cap and straight into my face!

Boyd, who had been watching, grabbed the lamp, closed the valve and pricked the jet clear of an obstruction, with a small bunch of wire that he carried for just such an eventuality. He then showed me how to ignite the gas, which was now hissing noisily from the jet. With a legerdemain worthy of a magician, he cupped his hand over the reflector and, drawing his palm rapidly over a flint-wheel on the rim, ignited the trapped gas with a most satisfying BANG! The result was a flame two inches long and of dazzling brightness. I had now learned one of the basic caving rituals.

The metallic smell of acetylene pervaded the atmosphere, making our noses tingle and somehow adding to the mystery of the cave nearby. I always find the smell of acetylene nostalgic. It must have the same effect as incense in religious rites, because although it has anaesthetic properties, it seems to raise my heartbeat in the expectation of adventures to follow.

By now we were all suitably clad, with lamps lit and ready to enter the cave. Boyd leading, we climbed over the entrance boulders and clambered down a slippery slope into a stream. The stream was quite swollen due to recent rains and ran through a deeply cut channel in the cave below. The shock of the cold water on my shins was immediate and as we waded further into the cave a deeper ache of cold developed in my feet and shinbones.

We moved quickly, the noise of our progress echoing eerily in the confined passageway. The chill cold members propelling me became icily numb, but I soon forgot them as I concentrated on trying to see where I was going. The thick fog of my breath kept obstructing my vision and I found that exhaling to one side was the only way to get a clear view ahead. Luckily my lamp gave a good light, hissing quietly on my helmet, and I could see where Boyd put his feet to best advantage.

Soon we arrived at a series of sandbanks and were able to climb out of the water. I felt my legs warm up almost immediately and my boots began to squelch empty. Here the stream ran in deep grooves between the banks and we stepped across these in places where they meandered. Eventually we were forced to stoop by the descending roof of what Boyd described as a 'bedding plane.' This was rather like a large edition of the black layer in a liquorice allsort with the roof and floor as the white bits. Sandy's height was a disadvantage here and in some places he had to crawl on all fours. Eventually we entered a boulder-strewn chamber where there were some old mine workings. We avoided these by crawling around to one side to gain a high passage where the going was easy.

I began to feel at home. The lights, the general chatter and the airy atmosphere seemed less threatening than the gloomy entrance. Besides, the water in my boots had warmed up. We paused by a low tubular passage on the right and Boyd explained that it connected to 'Darby Gill' *(Once again I misheard him. I later found out that it was Douber Ghyll, but that's another story)*. Doug and Sandy explored the passage for a short distance and I could hear their conversation echoing into a larger cavity. Boyd shouted for them to return and we continued along the main passageway.

Another chamber followed and then I was subjected to 'Hobson's Choice.' This was an upward wriggle and squeeze through a tumbled mass of boulders well lubricated by mud and a descending flow of icy water. I managed to keep fairly dry, but it was not very pleasant and I was glad to be able to stand up again on the other side. Sandy became very entangled in Hobson's. The problem was that his long legs had not finished turning one bend before his body was required to turn in a different direction at the next bend. With shouted advice and some pushing from Doug he was manoeuvred through, eventually emerging considerably wetter than I had.

With more scrambling and crawling, we eventually entered a high, narrow, passage. I learned that this was called a rift and that it had been cut in the limestone by the action of the flowing water. The rift led to a waterfall that we all managed to climb with ease. Further on, another waterfall cascaded from high in the roof. The ascent of this was more demanding. We placed our backs against one wall of the rift and our feet on the other wall. Using our leg muscles to press our backs into the wall, we could wedge our bodies to maintain position vertically. A slight release of pressure on the feet accompanied by an upward push of the arms and shoulders against the back wall allowed a steady if energetic ascent of the rift. I managed to keep away from the water and 'back and footed' high above it.

Overhead I could see large stalactites in the roof. Below these I could see Boyd standing on a ledge above the waterfall lip. It was a great comfort to have him above as a guide to shout instructions where the handholds were and I was soon able to join him. We waited for Doug and Sandy to arrive and then climbed further up into the roof. At one point I had to perform one or two rather hairraising manoeuvres over blackness that gave me a feeling of vertigo. Luckily the way became safer after these and we slid and crawled along a route that led to the finely decorated 'Roof Gardens.' I had never seen stalactites and stalagmites in their natural state before. My home territory of Buckinghamshire had no natural caves, so this was quite a revelation. Although they looked so easy to pick, I was told not to touch them—my first lesson in cave conservation. It was decided that this was a good place to stop and admire the view.

Each of us had secreted a chocolate bar in our helmet. These were now consumed as a mouthwatering source of energy. We had now been underground for nearly two hours and our stomachs confirmed that breakfast had been long ago. Soon I began to feel the coldness again. Boyd stood up, and we began to retrace our route to the entrance. The climb down the rift was less energy consuming, but rather more frightening than the ascent. Descending climbs are always more difficult than ascending ones. However, I managed to slither and brake my way down without mishap.

Ignoring my cold feet, wet behind, bruised knees and elbows, I felt reassured that I could cope with this new sport. I also began to enjoy the scenery now that my pupils had dilated and become accustomed to the dark. Even Hobson's Choice seemed facile on the return, although Sandy nearly lost his hammer in its confines. As we neared the entrance I smelt the sweet scent of the outside air well before the first signs of daylight. Several cavers have described this scent in words more eloquent than mine, but after several hours underground it always excites the nostrils. I always think how odd it is that we cannot smell this scent once we have been on the surface for a while. Near the entrance the perfume was particularly floral and redolent of summer meadows.

When we finally emerged into the warm sunlight, refreshed and satisfied with our exploits, I decided that I enjoyed caving. The pleasure and exhilaration of our recent adventure suppressed all thoughts of the long walk home. Life had taken a new turn and although I did not realise it at the time, my way of caving had begun.

2

The Eightfold Way of Caving

What is caving? Caving is fun. Caving is in the darkness. Caving is illuminating. Caving is dangerous. Caving is a minority sport for idiots. Caving is international. Caving is a muddy pastime. Caving warms you up. Caving gives you hypothermia. Caving is a sport for the individual. Caving is for everyone. Caving is exploration. Caving refreshes the soul. Caving is a way of life.

The human vocabulary, however large it may be, cannot describe everything completely and caving is no exception. Caving is a sport practised by cavers that is performed underground in naturally occurring limestone for pleasure or for scientific purposes. This rather cold description although capable of elaboration and further analysis conveys only relative knowledge. Absolute knowledge and understanding comes only to the practitioner. The noncaver finds it hard to understand what caving is all about and cavers themselves are often unaware of the full extent of the phenomenon.

The caving phenomenon consists of a continuous cycle of eight basic activities. Unlike the Eightfold Way of the Buddhists that leads to Enlightenment, the caving cycle is a closed loop and enlightenment comes only after many circuits. Even then it occurs in a different dimension. For most people the caving cycle is akin to *Samsara*, the cycle of birth and death, but to a few there is awakening—*Nirvana*.

The first stage of the caving cycle is the preparation stage. This is where plans are made, equipment assembled, rendezvous agreed, and underground routes decided. This stage is often conducted in a public house where creative thinking is assisted by regular doses of bitter beer. To many cavers the first stage is one of expectations where ideas flow and dreams float in the mind's eye.

The second stage involves travelling to the cave. Depending on the location of the cave in relation to the home territory, it can consist of anything from a short walk to a flight half way around the world. The last part of the journey is usually the most difficult as anyone who has sought an entrance on a misty moor or in a jungle will confirm. Cave entrances are sometimes very small and well hidden. They have no nameplates and often look very much alike so it is easy to enter the wrong cave even if an entrance is found. The second stage requires more organisation than most cavers are prepared to contribute and a rendezvous on time at the right place is often frustrated by the lost or latecomers.

The third stage of the caving cycle is to protect the body from the cave environment. The cavers change into their personal caving garments, selected for dry or wet conditions, pull on their boots or wellies, place protective helmets on their heads and then, if necessary, festoon themselves with climbing harnesses. Tackle bags are filled with rope, ladders and other caving equipment. Sufficient food and lighting supplies must also be carried to last the duration of the trip and cover emergencies. The communal equipment is shared out and packed in correct order for use underground. Lamps are tested, bootlaces tightened, harnesses adjusted and the thousand and one essential details completed. The weather is discussed and all sorts of minor complications occur which cause procrastination. By this time, most of the team is eager to get underground, and find the delays extremely aggravating. Nevertheless, caving is a serious undertaking and stage three is skimped at one's peril.

The fourth stage is the stage for which all cavers live. The fourth stage takes place underground. This stage is the top step of the stairway to the edge of the unknown. It is also the revitalisation stage that enables the caving cycle to continue. Many cavers leave the caving cycle because this fourth stage loses its effect on them and their ability to sustain energy and enthusiasm within the cycle. Here the caver leaves the everyday world behind and becomes immersed in a pattern of movement and thought that totally occupies the mind to the exclusion of all else. The sights, scents and sounds are experienced at many levels depending on previous caving and mindset. The adept can float along the most difficult passages, eyes and feet in perfect coordination, barely touching the rocks and wasting the minimum of energy on progression. This ease of movement allows the mind to concentrate on the total experience of being in a different world.

The fourth stage begins as the entrance portals are passed, includes the period of exploration that follows and ends with reemergence at the surface. Exploration is sometimes a euphemism for getting lost, digging in mud, carrying awkward loads in confined spaces, or for rigging and derigging pitches. The scientific pursuits such as cave photography, surveying, biological specimen hunting, and blasting obstructions can also take place at this stage. The duration of activities can vary from as little as a few hours to several days depending on the length and severity of the system visited. Eventually the team surfaces, and the fifth stage, the reverse of the interminable third stage, is completed. The cavers who can change into dry clothes the most quickly are the first to enter the sixth stage and can bag the best places in the pub. The sixth or refreshment stage is rarely short. A long caving trip develops an enormous thirst in cavers whose body fluids are depleted by perspiration. These lost liquids need replenishment as soon as possible. Later, hunger too sets in and needs allaying. The sixth stage is celebratory, enjoyed by all classes of caver and even by associated noncavers, depending on the hostelry involved. The best celebrations always include alcohol, a fire and music. This stage can often link with stage one as discussions about the completed trip inevitably suggest a followup. Sometimes the celebrations are so long and alcoholic that all memories, good and bad, are erased completely so that the effect on stage one planning is minimal.

The seventh stage of the caving cycle is often overlooked, even though it is the journey home. The caver is usually tired, and sometimes suffering from the effects of alcohol at this stage, so it can be fatal. If in doubt, the journey home should be delayed. This will lengthen the celebrations and fill the pockets of those clubs and pubs that rent out overnight accommodation.

The final stage in the eightfold way of caving is the maintenance stage. This applies to the caver as much as to his equipment. Both must be cleaned and mended and prepared for the next cycle. Failure here can limit future enjoyment unless torn muscles, blisters, failing lights or soleless boots are repaired. Stage eight is a rather tedious but necessary stage, especially if ropes are used. Anyone who has scrubbed a hundred-metre muddy rope will testify to this. Those who have scrubbed several hundred-metre ropes will wonder how it was that their companions avoided this part of the cycle!

The caving cycle cannot be dismissed without reference to the environment in which it is performed. Apart from society and surface scenes, the caves themselves have an incredible variety of experiences to offer. In some respects a cave is like a piece of music, available for interpretation and performance according to the ability of the artist. Although only the experts can tackle some caves, there is a wide range of choice to suit all abilities. The resulting experiences can be melodic or discordant depending on the match between the grade and the performer.

A recent press article posed the question: "Why do cavers continue exploring caves, when the ones that they find look the same as the others found before?" What a misconception! It is akin to saying that all Chinese look alike! Like a person, each cave has a distinct character of its own...sometimes benign, sometimes dangerous—depending on the season. Each has a basic structure and content that can be readily identified by the more perceptive observer. Using the brain and the five senses, there are many dimensions to explore. No one can deny the beauty, the challenge, the complexity and the sport provided by the caves, nor that caves contain some of the last unexplored territory on our planet. All caves are different from each other and the choice of cave environment is enormous. In addition, the exhilaration of discovering a new cave, or a new passage in a known cave, has to be experienced to be believed.

With this vast and varied world in which to perform the caving cycle, it is surprising that some cavers abandon it for a more ordinary life on the surface. Perhaps other sports seem more attractive—or else those who leave were only superficially involved in the first place. In any case, the caves and caving cycle are always there, providing a world for anyone to explore or to revisit over the passage of the years. Caving is like the sea: some folk dip their toes in, some paddle or swim, and others use it for travelling to distant shores.

3

Agen Allwedd

"Aggy", or Agen Allwedd, was the first large cave system that I explored as a leader. I had heard about its discovery whilst on National Service and had been told that it was near Llangattock in South Wales. This was to me a remote part of the world that I did not know and had never visited. However, I decided that I would go there as soon as I could. Soon after my demob and when I had settled back home in Buckingham, I bought a map of the area and made plans to go and investigate. I also discussed the matter with my friend Don who owned a large motorcycle. Don had never heard of caving before, but was game to accompany me if it promised some fun. The result was that one Friday we loaded camping and caving gear on to the bike and roared westwards up the Tingewick road to Oxford and then through Gloucester and Abergavenny to the South Wales village of Llangattock.

The map did not show Agen Allwedd, but from Llangattock we could see some limestone cliffs on the hill high above the village. We aimed for these, taking the road in the direction of Beaufort. Near the brow of the hill we crossed a cattle grid and turned left down a rough track littered with rocks and loose stones into a grassy valley. Here we decided to camp by a small stream in the lee of a stone wall. Don parked the bike out of sight and we went to seek camping permission.

Smoke was rising some distance away in a clump of trees, so we walked towards it and eventually arrived at a rather decrepit farmstead. The owner was quite friendly and we could just interpret his rich Welsh accents sufficiently to understand that we could camp on our chosen site provided that we did not light a fire. We bid him goodbye and returned to pitch the tent and prepare a meal before dark.

After dinner Don and I sat with our backs against the stone wall smoking our pipes and exchanging a few words in the peace of the evening. Suddenly a most peculiar noise shattered the silence. It sounded as if some large animal was being tortured. The caterwauling rose and fell and then ceased as suddenly as it had begun. We thought that we could hear voices, so decided to stroll down the valley and see what was happening.

In among the trees we could see the flicker of firelight and the silhouettes of people moving about. It was a scout camp! As Don and I walked up to the fire the scouts made us welcome. There seemed to be at least a dozen of them. Scattered around their tents we could see caving lamps and helmets. We enquired if they knew where Agen Allwedd was. Of course they did! It was the reason that they were camping there! They gave us clear instructions of how to find the entrance. It was at the end of an old tram road, reached by a steep path up through the thickets on the hill above the camp. They also told us how to find the way into the cave as far as 'Baron's Chamber.' They warned us of the tortuous 'Sally's Alley' at the entrance and the dangerously loose 'First Boulder Choke' which had to be negotiated to reach the chamber. We returned to our tent for an early night in the certain knowledge that tomorrow we would venture underground.

The next morning we rose early, ate a hearty breakfast, and put on our caving clothes. Don had his plumber's bib and brace worn over a jumper and old trousers. I had my old army denims and 'Long-johns.' Both of us had carbide lamps. Mine was mounted on my papier-mâché helmet acquired from the army. Don's was tied on to his motorcycle helmet with a complex network of string. I packed an old army haversack with matches, candles, spare carbide, a water bottle and some chocolate. After securing our tent, we took the steep path uphill through the scrub and bracken to the tram road. Puffing from the exertion, we paused at the top to admire the view over Crickhowell and the valley below. We then followed the track to the end where there was a small limestone face that contained an obvious keyhole-shaped entrance. Don remarked that it looked rather small and I had to admit that it was not what I expected, but then I had very little experience of such things. We filled our lamps with water from the water bottle and soon had them alight. I inserted myself into the upper, round part of the keyhole and wriggled forwards. Don bravely followed me in without comment, grunting with the strain of wriggling on his stomach, an activity to which he was unaccustomed.

The entrance crawl was quite arduous. It really was shaped like a keyhole! The round tubular part, just large enough to take our bodies, was slippery and in some places quite tight. As an added problem, the slot below was just the right width to trap boots and knees. Forward progress involved expending a considerable amount of energy. Our puffing and grunting filled the tube with noise and when we stopped for a rest a deep thumping sound could be heard. It was our hearts beating! The tube went from side to side and up and down, forcing us into the most complicated manoeuvres. Eventually the tube widened a little and the floor lowered to lead us into the 'Tool Chamber' where we could stand upright and collect ourselves together. To the left we could see a passage that the scouts had told us to avoid. It apparently led to a mud sump connecting with Ogof Gam, a small cave a few yards along the tram road from the entrance that we had taken. The connection was being excavated as evidenced by an ancient bucket and a spade propped against the wall. Perhaps one day the rigours of 'Sally's Alley' would no longer be necessary. Don voiced the opinion that caving seemed rather strenuous, but that now he could stand up he would rather continue than suffer Sally's Alley for a while! I was pleased to discover that he was not claustrophobic.

We took the obvious route to the right into a passage that forced us to stoop low. This was followed by a left turn where we had to crawl for some distance until the passage gained in size and we could walk upright again. Soon the passage became much larger and we climbed up to traverse over a narrow rift that led into a region where we had to climb over large rocks, at about fifteen feet or so above the floor. A small stream flowed in this part of the cave and we refilled our lamps from it before going over the top. After more up and down scrambling we came to a boulder-strewn chamber where we could see a short piece of 'electron' ladder belayed for a descent through a small hole between the rocks. We squeezed down this into the base of the boulders. At the bottom the route was hard to find, but a few twists and turns among the boulders and an obvious passage could be seen straight ahead. However, this was a key move that the scouts had warned us about. The correct way was hidden under a low sill to the left. Having located this, we slithered down a small elliptical tube into the stream again. We then continued forwards into what was obviously the beginning of the 'First Boulder Choke.'

The 'First Boulder Choke' was a complex jumble of large rocks with several alternative routes to choose. One route seemed to be more well-worn than most so we followed this on our knees as it was rather low. We crawled and wriggled among the boulders until we reached a neatly shaped crawl. The left-hand wall was smooth and semicircular. The right-hand side was of loose rocks jammed together and luckily of such a size as not to collapse onto us. At the end of this section there was an enlargement and we could see a way down amongst the boulders.

However, the route downwards seemed rather unstable and looking upwards I could see a length of chain hanging down. The chain passed through a most hazardous looking choke of loose rocks—some tied together with old army telephone cable. Pulling on the chain to avoid touching the poised boulders, I climbed gingerly upwards, selecting footholds with the utmost care. Don wisely remained in the safer confines of the crawl. He was proving to be an apt pupil and was weathering the rigours of caving without complaint. At the top there was a larger passage, so I shouted to Don to climb up and join me. The echo of my voice made me turn in surprise. There was obviously something large ahead, so I followed the route to the left and into the top of what was, to me, an unexpectedly enormous chamber. We had reached the 'Baron's Chamber.' Don joined me and we sat for a few minutes at the crest of a descending slope to adjust our lights and to congratulate ourselves on our route finding.

With our lamp flames at maximum length, we strode down the magnificent passageway over large banks of hard mud, covered with deep cracks and crevices, following a faint path uphill and down dale. Soon we came to a dip in the passage where there was a hole in the right hand wall and signs of a campsite. As the going was so easy we decided to continue along the main passage and after a few minutes' rapid progress came to another dip in the floor, again with a right hand passage. At this point we decided that we would halt, as our progress had been much better than we had expected. We sat down on a convenient mud-bank and ate some chocolate whilst discussing the return journey.

Once we were refreshed, we started back along the main chamber. However, at the first dip in the passageway, we decided to go down the hole in the floor to see where it went. We discovered that it led down to a wide stream-way. Here we paused to top up our lamps with water. What an exciting place! We could not resist exploring downstream, so we abandoned our plans to return and followed the lure of the stream. There was a large inlet passage on the right, but we decided to follow the main stream. Over the rocks, between the rocks and under the rocks, the stream-passage seemed to go on endlessly. We continued until the flames on our lights began to dim and we had to stop to recharge with carbide. By now we had been underground for three or four hours and since we only had a limited supply of carbide, we decided to stop further exploration and make tracks for the entrance again.

On the way back upstream we almost missed the route up to the Main Chamber and at the 'First Boulder Choke' we had some difficulty in finding the correct route, but otherwise our journey out was uneventful. Soon we were in the grip of 'Sally's Alley' and could smell the outside air. By now Don was quite tired and a bit bruised, but very keen to return for further exploration. He could see the attraction of caving in spite of the obstacles and physical demands. We wriggled out into the afternoon, sweaty, muddy and damp, but exhilarated by what we had found. It was certain that Aggy held lots of sport for the future.

In the years that followed, Aggy provided me and my caving friends with several weekends of enjoyable caving. During a series of visits, we followed most of the passages as far as they went. We found the way through 'The Second Boulder Choke' to reach a major stream-way deep in the cave. Unfortunately both ends of this stream-way ended in deep pools that we could not pass. On several occasions I camped in the valley alone when my companions failed to turn up. One such time, in the evening, after a solo trip to the second boulder choke, I saw lights on the tram-road. Hoping for company, I shouted and raced uphill to find that it was the British Nylon Spinners Caving Club. The next day they took me in with them on a digging trip and I managed to obtain a copy of their club journal with a survey of the recently discovered 'Summertime' series which was the other side of the large pool upstream called Turkey Pool.

A succession of longer trips followed over the Turkey Pool and into the Summertime Series. The crossing of Turkey Pool, reputed to be virtually bottomless, was always exciting. In our old 'Long-johns' and overalls we were not equipped for total immersion and had to traverse the pool on minute protrusions just below the surface. The most diffi-cult manoeuvre was always at the far side where a swing and a jump were required over the last deep section. Many of my friends fell in and survived a wetting, but I always managed to pass unscathed and it was not until wetsuits became available that I discovered that the pool was only chest deep at the deepest point! From then on familiarity bred contempt for what was originally a major obstacle.

We moved our campsite for these trips to 'Summertime' to a new base on the tramroad near a spring at the cave of Eglwys Faen. We also altered our approach route and approached from the far end of the tramroad via Brynmawr or up a steep hill from Llangattock. As I began to know the area better, we made several expeditions from the 'Old Daren Sunday School,' a small cottage at the road-head. The 'Old Daren Sunday School' provided a relatively comfortable base, particu-larly in the cold and typically wet weather of the region. During this period Ogof Gam was connected to the Tool Chamber making the entrance much less arduous.

We also began to arrive by car. This made travelling to the region easier and faster. This was quite beneficial as, even with the easier access via Ogof Gam, some of our trips underground were quite long and a trip of twelve hours to the far corners of 'Summertime' was not unusual. During a week of caving one winter we lost a complete day as our time underground became out of phase with the twentyfour hour day on the surface.

I had an enforced rest from Aggy visits when my work took me to Teesside for a period of about eight years. On my eventual return to the South I renewed my acquaintance. I found that several new pas-sages had been discovered and I was able to complete the 'Grand Cir-cle' going downstream from Turkey junction and through the third and fourth boulder chokes, that had been penetrated after extensive digging, to return via the arduous Southern Stream Passage. The Nature Conservancy now controlled access and the entrances had been fitted with padlocked gates. The Chelsea Caving Club had acquired 'White Walls' at the end of the tramroad and I often accepted their generous hospitality and made several trips with their members, often into new ground, using their facilities as a base.

Over the years I established a regular pattern of making a January tour of the 'Inner Circle.' I usually aimed to explore a different passage to the end on each visit, occasionally diverting to some other area as new explorations were made. The routes at the entrance became more polished and slippery. The main routes in the cave became very hard-packed and worn. Cavers relinquished Aggy for the delights of Daren Cilau and other nearby excitement, but I always enjoyed a trip in Aggy. Aggy, to me, has an eternal quality of its own and holds many memories of my early caving years that are relived at each visit.

My daughter Catherine's first visit to Aggy did not go as planned. We arrived at 'White Walls' one January afternoon to find it a hive of activity. Arthur, the hut warden, told us about a breakthrough in 'Gothic Passage' at the end of Southern Stream Passage and invited us to go and look at the new discoveries. Sniffing and wheezing with a heavy cold and unfit after the Christmas festivities, I did not fancy the rigours of Southern Stream Passage, but Catherine was so keen to visit new ground that I decided to make an effort. The pair of us set off for the cave clad in wetsuits and carrying a brand new tackle bag full of rope, spare lights and food. The entrance series posed no problems and I let Catherine ascend to Baron's Chamber first in the hope that she would recapture my own excitement on breaking out into Baron's Chamber for the first time. Recently returned from the large caverns of the Pierre Saint Martin in the Pyrenees, however, she was singularly unimpressed.

Whilst I regained my breath, Arthur, John and a party of Chelsea and Gloucester cavers overtook us. We followed them to the start of Southern Stream Passage and began our struggle downstream. The wretched tackle bag seemed to catch on every possible protrusion and I rapidly became hot and flustered. Catherine took the bag for a while, then we fought it together before leaving it at around the halfway mark. Another group of cavers overtook us, but by now I had burnt out some of my catarrh and was beginning to fire on all four cylinders. We came to the waterfall, a drop of about ten feet that had stopped me on my first visit to the passage decades ago. After some hesitation we gingerly climbed down, using small holds and jumped the last few feet to avoid a soaking. A short way past this point we started to look upwards for the high level Gothic passage. Luckily Arthur was surveying there and we saw his light shining in the roof. We easily located the way up to his survey point after crossing a traverse equipped with a hand-line.

A dry rift passage led to a Tee-junction. Left went to the 'Gloucester' series and right to the 'Chelsea' series. We took the right-hand passage. This soon lowered to a shattered looking crawl and a small squeeze. Soon we were in new ground. The walls glittered with small crystals and the sandy floor looked barely marked by human feet. We squeezed through a sandy constriction where I had to dig like a mole to get through and then came to a series of chambers connected by sandy crawls. Catherine was really enjoying herself and although I did not feel a bundle of energy, I did have a second wind in such pristine surroundings. It was very exciting to have the feeling of breaking new ground as only one or two cavers had been there before us.

We continued along the passage until we came to masses of crystal in the chamber ahead, thoughtfully taped off to avoid their destruction. In some places it was like being on the moon. Absolute silence reigned. A sandy, arid floor was soft beneath our feet. The black roof twinkled with small crystals. The whole area was virtually untouched and had only been seen by a handful of people so far. Catherine was the first woman in the series and at fifteen, certainly the youngest. Unfortunately I had made the mistake of taking my wristwatch. In distant passageways, particularly new ones like those we were passing through, time seems to stand still and it is common to return many hours beyond that anticipated. Now, however, the beeper reminded me that it was two o'clock.

We had to be back at 'White Walls' by 6 p.m. and since we had already been underground three hours or so we were obliged to return to avoid being overdue. Reluctantly we retraced our steps, leaving the Gloucester Series for another time. The Southern Stream passage seemed no less arduous on the way out, but we surmounted the waterfall easily and were soon grappling with the tackle bag again. At a convenient water inlet, I slaked by thirst, exacerbated by my heavy cold. The water tasted like nectar. On we went steadily if slowly until eventually we emerged in the Main Chamber where we stopped for a chat with a group completing the Grand Circle. The entrance series followed, for me as a habit, for Catherine as a surprise, and we emerged into the dark, the lights of Crickhowell twinkling below us through the strands of low cloud that were floating past us. Two other cavers who caught up with us helped to lighten the long walk back along the tramway. Soon we were back in the welcoming warmth of White Walls. Catherine certainly knew how to choose a first trip into Aggy; so much more spectacular than mine! I suppose that it's better to be born lucky than rich though, and I was glad that Aggy still had a thing or two up her muddy sleeve.

4

Sump One

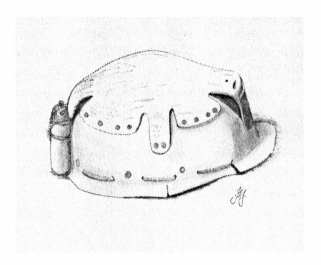

An old caving helmet

A fear of the water pervaded my childhood years; exactly what caused it I cannot tell, but deep pools along the river and gloomy black ponds and lakes always gave me the creeps. In those days there were no swimming pools in my neck of the countryside and the only bathing place was in the river, so I rarely went into the water except at bathtime. One year, the local church choir of which I was a junior member went on a coach trip to Banbury baths for the annual 'treat.' The neat metal steps into the water and the gently sloping floor of the swimming pool enticed me in, and for the first time I explored the shallows to the depth of my chin. Some of the older boys had brought a dinghy with them, which they inflated, for some extra fun. Along with several other trebles I was invited to participate in a short boat trip. Unsuspectingly we clambered in for a free ride, surprised that our erstwhile bullies were so bountiful. It was not until they had towed us out to the deep end that I realised to my horror that it was a trick! Roaring with laughter, they pulled out the bungs and as the air hissed out I abandoned ship and jumped out into the water. I now know how the unfortunate Egyptians must have felt when the Red Sea closed in over their heads! To this day I can still see the bluegreen walls of water collapsing in over me in slow motion. Water entered my mouth and nostrils...I choked and sucked in more...I thrashed around in a panicstricken attempt to swim, but it was of no use. With a dreadful nightmarish choking sensation overwhelming me I realised I was drowning. Luckily someone dragged me out and performed artificial respiration on me and soon I was gasping and breathing again. This traumatic event enhanced my fear of the water and for many years afterwards I avoided any similar encounters like the plague.

Some time after my voice broke, I left the choir and went camping with the Scouts at the seaside in Devon. In the relatively warm shallows, waist deep in the sea, I managed to teach myself to do the Dog Paddle. Gradually I conquered my fears and by my late teens I had progressed to swimming in the river and in a local mill pool where I even ventured out of my depth. As my confidence improved I actually began to enjoy the water, but I always had a healthy respect for it and occasionally some mishap would panic me again, albeit momentarily.

Many years later, after I had taken up caving, I had a short reminder of my subconscious fears. We had gathered in the Mendip village of Priddy at the Sandhurst Caving Club cottage for a descent of Swildon's Hole that was situated in a nearby field. What a watery cave it was! Although we tried hard to avoid a wetting by taking the 'Dry Way,' we all became soaked to the skin whilst descending 'The Forty Foot' wet pitch and even wetter after 'The Twenty'. I was, however, able to skirt

'The Double Pots' without falling in, unlike one of my luckless comrades, and was glad that we avoided further wetting by taking the 'Barnes' Loop' bypass. Eventually we reached the point where the water and roof met at Sump One.

The way on was under water for about six feet with no airspace. A daunting prospect! None of us had ever passed a sump before and we hesitated, desultorily pulling on the diving line which disappeared into the sump pool, whilst trying to decide who would go first. A suitable hero did not volunteer so our chattering teeth and shivering bodies decided for us that we had done well enough for a first trip and that a return to the surface was called for.

The next time that I visited Sump One I went in more determined company, and with the sole objective of reaching the passages on the far side of the sump. Barry, my companion, was an experienced caver from Yorkshire where at that time there were no freedivable sumps to tax his nerve. He was a really 'hard' caver and actually relished the idea of diving a sump.

We crouched on our haunches in the icy water, immersing our bodies gradually to overcome the loss of breath caused by the cold. Clad only in 'Long Johns' and cotton overalls, we found it difficult to gulp down enough air as the icy water shrank our lungs. Not a man to mess about, Barry soon decided that he had acclimatised. He rammed his sodden helmet firmly onto his head, took a deep breath, and plunged into the water, pulling on the diving line to hold himself down. A swirl of bubbles and he was gone!

I felt very alone, holding the line loosely so that he could signal when he was through. Three distinct pulls on the line. He was through! A momentary fear welled up inside me as I sank down in the freezing water, still finding it difficult to breathe. This was the moment of truth—it really was do or die! I could not leave Barry waiting on the other side. I breathed in and out two or three times to maximise my oxygen load, screwed my eyes and mouth tightly shut, ducked into the water and pulled on the rope as hard as I could.

The shock of the cold water was mind numbing. I was overwhelmed in the blackness. The water seemed quite deep, but my heels hit the roof once or twice so that I knew that I was full length in the sump. The whirl of my frantic movement, the pull of my muscles, the icy cold and the bursting sensation in my lungs aroused my atavistic terror of drowning. Pull! Pull! I could feel the water rushing past me as I hurtled through the sump. Clunk! My helmet was jammed in the roof! Horror! It's too tight! I struggled with all my might, panicstricken, thrashing about like a fish on a line. Suddenly my arm felt no resistance…Must be air…Spluttering and gasping I erupted from the sump pool and stood up.

I had passed the sump, crossed the pool on the other side and had been trying to drive my head into some rocks near the rope attachment point! Laughing at my obvious discomfort, Barry relit my carbide lamp for me and we paused to look at each other, soaking wet and frozen in the dim light.

"I didn't know that you enjoyed the water that much!" said Barry. "Let's go and see what's ahead before we both die of exposure!"

5

Popova Polje

When I was an undergraduate I joined the motley collection of individuals who comprised the university caving club. In those days caving was a rather happygolucky activity and nothing was ever organised except for trips during the vacations. These outings depended on the current membership, which changed annually and thus presented a fair selection from Yorkshire, Mendip and South Wales caves. One summer I was lucky enough to be invited to join a caving expedition to Montenegro, ostensibly as an experienced caver. (I had done Douber Ghyll passage!) Fabian, the expedition leader, had been to the region the year before and had established contact with the Karst Institute at Llublianja to provide us with caving guides who were a mandatory accompaniment for foreign cavers in Yugoslavia. Fabian had also acquired a Ford fifteen hundred-weight van that had been converted for transporting donkeys and would suit us admirably.

We gathered at Haywards Heath railway station, Martin and Stuart from Mendip, myself from the country, Tim from the mountains and Jared from America. Jared had little experience of caving, but was learning to play the violin, which he carried everywhere with him and insisted on playing at every opportunity. As the expedition wore on, his instrument escaped fracture only by dint of his imaginative hiding places for it when not in use. Fabian met us with the donkey truck and drove us to his house to collect the expedition equipment.

Most of the caving gear was conventional, 'Electron' ladders, hawser laid rope, a dinghy and suchlike, but the cooking equipment was most bizarre. As an erstwhile Boy Scout I was accustomed to neatly stacked billycans, mess tins and decent cutlery, so I was rather shocked to see the odd collection of rusty old saucepans, battered china plates, black frying pans and verdant cutlery that Fabian shook from a sack in his garage. There was even a runcible spoon! My education, however, was still incomplete. I found several thin cardboard boxes which had 'Kleenex' written on them and I opened one of these at the end to see what was inside. Perhaps it was a detergent? Unfortunately it only contained a set of tightly packed paper napkins. Later I declined to own up when the 'idiot' who had wrecked the tissue box was sought! I now know exactly how those nocturnal raiders of camp larders feel when they gnaw the soap.

The van was soon loaded, not forgetting two large tins of honey presented to us by Fabian's father who kept bees in his spare time. The tins had a length to diameter ratio of at least three to one, which could prove difficult for removing the last sticky spoonfuls. Fabian took his beekeeper's hat for when the sun came out and with tins of soup and plenty of money we set off on our journey.

After crossing the Channel, we drove in shifts with few stops except for essentials and Liege, Munich, Heiligenblut, and the Gross Glockner Pass rolled under our wheels until we reached the Yugoslav border. Tight entry restrictions were then in force, and all of us had to obtain visas beforehand, so we approached the Customs with some trepidation. The Yugoslav border guards looked extremely fearsome armed with wicked looking machine guns and leading ferocious muzzled guard dogs. We watched them dismantle the car and luggage of the unfortunate Italians in the queue ahead of us and wondered what they would do to the indescribable mess of gear in the back of our van. I could even imagine them sinking their arms to the elbows in our honey tins in search of contraband! However, we must have looked simple, or honest, or else the GB plates were a favourable icon because they let us through after a most cursory inspection.

We drove on to Llublianja and then to a small village called Rakek where our guides Andrej and Bostian met us. They both looked very fit and bronzed and, as well as speaking good English, were extremely friendly and hospitable. Andrej invited us home to dinner and after a few glasses of plum syrup and water, we sat down for the meal. Large platters were carried in, loaded with what I later learnt were stuffed peppers. I had never seen or eaten such food before, but it tasted delicious, the novel flavours permeating my mouth and nasal tissue and providing additional value far into the evening. For the dessert, a large plate of dumplings was placed on the table. We spooned several of these onto our plates and waited for the custard, but it was clear that we were expected to eat them on their own. Etiquette required us to do this, in spite of baulking at a mouthful of suet, but luckily we had a most pleasant surprise: each dumpling contained a sweet plum inside! The plate was soon emptied, withdrawn, and replaced by another plateful. The second plate was soon empty too and the same vanishing trick performed on several more platefuls until we could eat no more. We must have consumed enough sustenance for several days of hard travelling at one sitting. Eventually we left the table and all of us slept soundly, barely moving with our suet ballast.

The next day we drove south via Zagreb, Banja Luka and then past Jajce into the mountains where we camped overnight in a small village. Here we received further hospitality from the villagers in the form of grapes and 'Rakia,' a sort of home-made plum brandy. As we continued south the roads became very dusty and bumpy and it was not until we completely removed the canvas covers from the back of the van to let everything blow straight through that we could obtain any comfort.

Two days later we reached a small village called Zavala situated on the rim of an alluvial flood plain, or polje, encircled by mountains. Here we obtained permission to camp on the floor of the polje in among the fields of maize near a small spring. We learnt that in the late summer and autumn the polje flooded to such a depth that the maize had to be harvested by boat. This presumably accounted for the numerous ponds that were dotted about among the maize fields, so we were glad that the weather was fine and settled. The local shopkeeper sold everything that we needed, dispensing most of his goods from woven sacks into brown paper bags for our convenience. When we told him where we were to camp he made a noise like a motorbike. Andrej eventually explained…we were camping on Popova Polje.

Loaded with provisions, we drove on to the polje and located the campsite. We soon had the tents erected, petrol stoves alight and a meal in progress. After the rigours of the journey we were glad to settle down for a while. The next day dawned cloudless and sunny and we went caving.

Our objective was a large cave nearby called Vieternica—'The Cave of Winds.' This cave was reported to be thirteen kilometres long, but there had been an earth tremor recently and from the dust blown out of the cave mouth it was surmised that it might now be a lot shorter. We climbed up to the entrance, situated about half way up the hill near our camp and were confronted by a howling gale issuing from the cave mouth. The cave seemed aptly named and since the gale blew our carbide lamps out, we had to feel our way in along the walls of the entrance until we reached an enlargement where the draught abated somewhat. Once our lights were on full flame we could see that the entrance passage was quite large and well decorated. The going was easy, and we made rapid progress walking on a relatively flat floor for about half a mile until we came to a large lake.

On the shore we inflated our ancient RAF dinghy and Stewart, who was a strong swimmer, paddled off into the darkness towing a light cord so that we could pull the dinghy back for another transit. (The dinghy was only large enough for one person to sit in at a time.) A shout from Stewart, now out of sight in the blackness, echoed across the lake and we pulled on the towline until the dinghy snagged. The lake had an awkward bend in it and after some jiggling and pulling and combined tactics with Stewart's backpull line, we freed the dinghy which emerged yellow and silent out of the blackness like an eerie invitation to the underworld. Martin was next and off he paddled, only stopping halfway to blow up the dinghy which now had an audible leak in it. One by one we made our various ways across the lake, mostly without problems and with considerable usage of air until we had all gathered on the far shore.

Leaving the dinghy on the beach, we shouldered our haversacks and explored further on. The large galleries continued as before, leading past some huge dry sinter pans or dried up gour pools and into a very large chamber with a sandy floor. About half a mile further on we came to a massive boulder choke covered with spiky concretions and crystal formations. Here we could smell fresh rock dust from the recent roof fall. There were large slabs hanging from the roof here. Only after crawling past several of these we realised they were just loosely attached by one end to the roof. A careless push could bring the whole lot down! Our exploration of the enormous choke was made very cautiously from then on, but unfortunately we could not find a way through. Rather disappointed at our discovery, we made the long trek out intending to return the next day to survey and photograph the place before a final attempt to get into the passages reported to be beyond.

Over the next few days our forays revealed no progress and eventually we abandoned further explorations. I remember that I was the last person to cross the lake on the return—a memorable event. Standing alone on the inner shore, I pulled on the line. The dinghy began its last ferry trip. On the corner it became stuck. My heart raised a beat or two as I jiggled and tugged on the line. What relief to feel the line come free and to see the ancient yellow dinghy slide quietly across the lake and on to my silent shore. I know now how sailors must feel to see the lifeboat coming when they have been shipwrecked. I loaded my gear in and gently paddled off across the lake, peering back from the middle to take a last look at a shore that I have never seen since.

After Vieternica we explored further afield into caves suggested to us by the locals. Although we found nothing of significance, several interesting events happened to us. One cave descended steeply via several pitches and then petered out into a series of deep pools with minimal airspace above. I passed three of these 'ducks' before realising that noone was following me. My muffled shouts elicited no response so I returned to find the reason. It soon became painfully obvious…on my way in I had stirred something up in the first pool which smelt abominable! The others had decided to move back from it. Unfortunately for me the only way out was to flounder through it again! Two days later I developed a swollen knee and had to be rushed to a hospital for emergency treatment. Luckily I soon recovered and was able to participate in other explorations.

During our surface reconnaissance we had seen many large serpents basking in the sunshine, and since they had such a fearsome appearance we gave them a wide berth. I often wondered if they went inside the caves and what it would be like to meet one face to face in a crawl. Imagine my horror when in one very small cave near the village I rounded the corner of a tightish squeeze to be confronted by two eyes, glittering fiercely in the light from my lamp. I froze solid, the thought of a snakebite in the face crossing my mind. We stared at each other for what seemed an eternity. Then the toad, for that is what it was, obligingly hopped to one side out of my way! It was a minute before I could move again. Unfortunately the toad was not guardian of a large cavern or even any treasure, merely a maze of impenetrable fissures that defied further exploration.

One evening by the campfire, Andrej returned with something taken from the darkness around us. He placed it on the ground between cupped hands, inside the circle of firelight. As he let go, an enormous frog leapt out and shot at least four feet into the air in an enormous jump straight over Stewart's head. Howling with laughter, Andrej explained that the ponds were full of these enormous frogs and that in fact they were edible. A discussion followed and Bostian went off to catch a frog and put its edibility to the test. He soon returned. Apparently it was quite easy to attract the frogs using a bright light which seemed to hypnotise them to sit still long enough to be grabbed from behind. The second frog seemed larger than the first. With hind legs stretched out it measured almost a foot from head to toe. Bostian killed it by hitting its head on a rock and passed it nonchalantly to Andrej. Pulling out a large sheath knife, Andrej, who was training to be a doctor, neatly severed the unfortunate frog at the waistline. Throwing the upper half into the bushes, Andrej carefully pulled the skin off the large hind legs, rather like removing a small pair of trousers. A sharp jerk and the 'trousers' were off. The next step was to clean the legs for cooking. Andrej dropped the legs into a mess tin of salt water where they started to jerk about—a perfect example of swimming top-less! A small frying pan containing some olive oil was warmed on a petrol stove and the legs were then dropped in after a quick wipe with a handkerchief and fried until the surfaces became a golden brown. Andrej cut the connected legs apart and, taking a leg, proffered it for tasting. It looked nice, smelt nice and amazingly tasted nice! There was sufficient meat for all of us, including Jared who was a rather fastidious eater to conclude that frogmeat was delicious.

During the next day's caving we forgot the frogs, until returning to camp in the evening they reminded us by their gleeps and chirps that the polje was full of tasty food. We decided to have a frog feast. Each armed with a lamp, we crept up on the ponds and grabbed frogs with surprising ease, or at least for the first half dozen or so. The frogs remaining after our first sortie were not so stupid and we had to wait quietly for them to resurface with our lights covered and then suddenly shine our lights and grab quickly. The final corpses were obtained by hurling sticks and rocks at the rapidly moving targets as our hunt degenerated into a less elegant full-frontal attack on the unfortunate amphibians. Back at the camp we cut off the hind legs and debagged numerous frogs so that we soon had a large saucepan full of swimming legs—a weird sight indeed! Two frying pans were heated on the fire and a tasty meal was prepared. With salad, bread and plenty of wine the frogs' legs tasted superb, hot and sizzling from the pans with a touch of garlic added at the last minute.

As we lounged back in the firelight, our lips and fingers covered in garlic-flavoured oil, I pondered how pleasant our detour from civilisation had been and wondered what next year's tadpoles would think of our exploits!

6

Saint Catherine's to Fisherstreet

Doolin
Beautiful Grotto

County Clare at Easter is usually sunny with the occasional refreshing nip in the air and rarely wet. A welcome rest from the hustle and bustle of city life, the leisurely lifestyle takes a few days to acclimatise to when caving in the low-lying limestones near the Atlantic coast. Although the caves of the region lack verticality and the passages are often narrow and sinuous, each has a charm of its own. Polnagollum, Poulelva, PolanIonian, Faunarooska, Doolin, the Cullauns and Coolagh River cave—their Irish names tripped from our tongues as easily as their mud from our wetsuits in the nearby sea. The mighty cliffs of Moher, the mysterious Burren and Slieve Elva seemed key features in a landscape embedded with small bars and homely villages where the eyes and ears mellowed with the green and golden magic of ancient times. When the curraghs slip in on the tide from the Aran Isles and the quiet men arrive to sit in the bar after buying their paraffin from the village store, it is easy to understand the local legends of leprechauns and elves. Peat fire smells, cheap steak and creamy Guinness are more easily remembered than the underworld and readily recaptured in the earthy tang of Irish whiskey.

Our first visit to the area was in Trevor's ancient Hillman Husky. Chris, Dilys and I were crammed inside with the necessary gear piled on top of us to travel all the way from England in some discomfort. We stayed at the Ritz Hotel in Lisdoonvarna. Although it was closed for the season, we were able to rent rooms for a small payment. We slept in sleeping bags in the vacant bedrooms and cooked communal meals in the huge kitchen with the rest of our club. Buck, John and Elsie, Wally and Jane, Mick and Sue, Aubrey, Lol with his guitar and many others, all of us drawn by the caves and country. Our evenings in Gus O'Connor's bar at Fisherstreet were always tuneful, the local flutes and pipes and spoons providing accompaniment to our voices lubricated by the creamy brew and something stronger. Of all our trips below ground, however, the underground traverse of the Doolin system from St Catherines swallet to the Fisherstreet pothole near Gus O'Connor's bar remains the most memorable.

We began with a late start and drove down to Fisherstreet where the pitch into the cave system was located in a field not far from Gus O'Connor's. Without changing into caving gear we rigged the pitch with electron ladder for our eventual exit and then drove inland to St Catherine's swallet. After changing into our underground 'grots,' we cavers left our clean clothes in the cars and then our wives drove them back to Gus O'Connors to await our arrival later in the day. With three or four hours of fun ahead of us, we gathered by the entrance and began clearing away the flood debris to gain access.

A low crawl led to a short squeeze, only a problem for the larger members of our party, and then the passage continued to a sudden enlargement where we could stand up. The complex of junctions that followed is hard to remember, except that it led to a series of chambers. One called 'The Smithy' was particularly well decorated and 'The Beautiful Grotto' had a calcite pillar with long lines of thin straw stalactites running along the cracks in the ceiling. After taking photographs, we continued downstream in a narrow passageway armed with razor-sharp rock flakes that could cut the shins and thighs of careless cavers. An easy option to the right led into the Great Oxbow, a gallery about four feet wide and twenty feet high with a dark flat ceiling high above and orange and white flowstone ribs like small curtains running down the walls.

By now the photographers in our group were delaying our progress, but we continued down a steepening descent and some small cascades as the passage narrowed and the roof lifted until we were in the Great Canyon. Several deep pools here provided a refreshing wetting before the next obstacle, the Great Boulder Fall. Here we had to climb up past more razorsharp flakes and then find various ways up and down to reach the stream again. However, a further climb up high over the boulders to a well decorated grotto enticed our photographers off route for a while and so we spent some time regrouping before proceeding downstream again.

The roof became lower as we progressed downstream and we took an oxbow to avoid crawling in the water in an area where my memories are vague, but the next landmark was soon reached, the Aran View passage. The dark and gloomy tributary from the Aran View swallet entered from the right at the same roof level but running in at about kneelevel. The passage crosssection flattened out across the limestone beds just past this junction, but after some distance lifted again and we were soon scurrying under the Aille cascades that poured in overhead, presumably leaking from the Aille river on the surface. We ducked and hurried under the deluge to avoid its full force and made our humid way past more showerbaths until we were forced to stop and crawl in another low bedding plane half full of water.

We knew that we were now very near to the Fisherstreet pothole, and soon we could glimpse daylight through the small airspace between the low roof and the water. Wallowing and splashing along in the current, we floundered our various ways through to the bottom of the pothole where our ladder was hanging. It was not a particularly comfortable spot to linger in so we wasted no time in climbing out to the surface where the sun was shining.

We had all enjoyed a most refreshing trip, apart from the odd cuts and bruises. It did not take us long to de-tackle the pitch and, once the ladder and ropes had been stowed into a plastic sack, we walked across the field to Gus O'Connor's bar. Here we tapped on the windows to attract the attention of our wives, who were comfortably ensconced within. They came to the door to see us and we managed to acquire a pint of Guinness apiece with the admonition to drink outside as we were too muddy to come in—a most refreshing and intoxicating finale to our traverse!

The muddy glasses were handed back empty and then we squelched down to the seashore for a swim. The sea was icy cold but our wetsuits kept us warm. Only our exposed hands suffered. The mud washed off easily in the surf and soon we were all bouncing up and down in the waves further out in a final swim like playful seals, before returning to change into warm clothes. How many underground traverses end as delightfully as this? What Doolin lacks in length and depth is amply repaid by its surface trimmings, which must add to its status among the world's most enjoyable traverses.

7

The Unknown

Canal on Mars

Deep future ahead and tomorrow around the corner, the hours and days mapped by our plans and expectations, we are all on an expedition into the unknown whether we realise it or not. Nourished by our dreams and guided by our experiences we follow a path, hopefully forwards, surmounting the obstacles that we encounter like cavers underground. Some routes are complex, some simple, some arduous and some delightfully easy, but time passes remorselessly so that we can never retrace our steps except in our memories. For many people the present is a mere rehearsal for the future, like practising on a climbing wall, or following well-known routes as a training exercise. The adept, however, can voyage through the present and into the unknown, the excitement sustained as far as stamina and faculties allow.

The caver has two unknowns to contend with, the caves and himself. Considering the caves first; there are the caves that others know but are as yet unknown to the caver himself; and then there are the undiscovered caves known to 'no-one'. Even familiar caves can present an unknown face. A sudden flood, an earth tremor, surface activities or erosion can transform a benign cave into a frightening adversary. Loose rocks, slippery slopes and crumbling handholds are unknowns to contend with even on familiar territory. The exploration of a cave for the first time, even if it has been previously discovered and explored by others, is a voyage into the unknown. Although its passageways may have been mapped and named, until they have been perceived in person they are not known in the true sense and often prove how weak the models in the mind's eye can be.

The ultimate unknown, the new cave or passage where no one has been before, is the main objective of most cavers. An indescribable feeling of the numinous accompanies such explorations. The pristine mud or sand, never seen or touched before, is changed forever by the imprints of the explorer's boots. The wonder and excitement that last so fleetingly for the discoverers are often shared to a lesser extent by subsequent explorers, even though there is only one true breakthrough.

Most new cave discoveries are expected, usually following an assault on a promising lead derived from local or geological knowledge. These discoveries represent the expected unknown. The most exciting discoveries, however, are those that are completely unexpected and made by cavers blessed with serendipity. A sudden rockfall or a flood reveals a new hole, a caver spots a hitherto unnoticed draught, or an intimidating boulder ruckle is found to have an easy way through it. No one knows where the next such prize will come from, nor how many caverns remain to be discovered. This unknown potential is the very heart of caving, the powerful force of the underground.

Now to consider the unknowns in the caver himself. Many cavers gain selfknowledge from the practice of caving and many noncaving unfortunates are herded into caves to seek themselves on 'character building' courses by those with little regard for the value of personal choice in such issues. In trying to discover ourselves we often think that we are fully aware of what we know and what we do not know. However this is a delusion; any friend or artist can soon reveal to us knowledge that we possess or lack that previously we were unaware of. The extent of our ignorance nearly always requires an external trigger, and caves are good prompters. Like the caves, our familiar selves have unknown aspects which can be revealed or changed by sudden events or environmental assault. The interplay of cave and caver allows an interchange to take place between reality and imagination from which awareness and selfknowledge springs. Those who follow the sport of their own free will are rarely untouched by their discoveries, the friends that they meet, or the experiences that they undergo in pursuit of their chosen lifestyle.

We often imagine that the unknown can be tamed by the application of a suitable name. Whilst there is no doubt that naming something fixes it in our minds and, to a certain extent, alters our perception of it, the thing itself remains unchanged. Names can provide a useful handle for reference purposes, but the name can sometimes mislead and hide important aspects of the thing that is named. Names mean different things to different people. In addition, a name often reveals something of the namer from the synergy between the observer and the observed. The names of caves and of cavers provide many interesting examples of these points.

When a cave is first discovered, it is difficult to describe it without naming its key features. The early cave explorers, in deciding the key features and choosing names for them, often reveal more about themselves than about the cave. The commonest names derive from the cavers' literary knowledge. For example, Tolkein's fantasy novels inspired many cave explorers who left a trail of Hobbit and Elvish words throughout the underworld. The more explicit names for obvious features like a squeeze, a duck, a hole or a particular speleothem are often differentiated by the addition of the explorer's name. 'Hardy's Horror,' 'Bob's Pit,' 'Idiot's Leap,' and 'Peter's Pretty Passage' are a few examples of this. Other names have been derived from the explorer's taste in pop music, local dialect, scientific knowledge, or even his favourite beer. The surprising thing is that after continued usage, the names really begin to generate a feeling for what was intended.

Nicknames are another example of attempting to define an unknown. Most caving clubs have a few good examples, although some clubs seem to have more than others do. The simplest nicknames are adjectival. 'Squeaky Dave,' 'Big Jane,' and 'Salford Phil' are typical examples, with 'Bungalow Bill' and 'Talking Terry' in a more alliterative style. Then there are the animal names such as 'Mouse,' 'Moose,' 'Slug,' 'Pooh' and 'Le Rat.' The practical sounding names like 'Wingnut,' 'Lugger,' 'Tipple,' 'Joppo,' 'Trapper' and 'Dusty' are counterbalanced by the more esoteric 'Buddha,' 'Plato' and 'Loofah.' Considering the fact that all of these nicknames apply to real people, it would be interesting to know exactly how the names were derived and by whom!

Sometimes it is better to avoid using names. In fact, something unknown is not always to be feared. The unknown can be a considerable asset in certain circumstances. "Ignorance is Bliss" rings true. For example it is an advantage when climbing over a 'bottomless' pit not to be able to see the bottom. The unseen depth is less of a drain on the nervous system than the same drop clearly visible in the open air. Constrictions, squeezes, ducks and sumps are often passed more easily if encountered without previous knowledge or forethought. For many years I sidled down the 'Crab Walk' in Giants Hole, Derbyshire without any bother. Then one day someone asked me if I had had any problems in passing 'The Vice'…On my next trip I managed to become stuck in it! Unnamed, I had no slot in my memory for it; named, it became an obstacle to be overcome well before I entered the cave. The unknown is thus not always a cause of fear or inhibition.

Mankind has survived by adaptation to change, but as a result most individuals are resistant to change and are constrained by social pressures to adopt what is considered to be 'Normal' behaviour. There is a desire to control change or even to prevent it from occurring. This arises from the fear of the unknown.

However, everything that we encounter is susceptible to change whether we like it or not. The unknown results of change are always around to produce unexpected pleasure or horror. Farmers can improve moor drainage to render benign caves violent in a sudden downpour. A new climbing gadget can make the ascent of long rope pitches easy, but the result of not knowing how to place the rope to prevent it from fraying could well be fatal. The unknown is always lurking in the familiar environment and should never be forgotten.

For novice cavers of unknown capabilities, the exploration of what they can achieve in wellknown cave systems provides considerable pleasure. As they progress, their demands for greater challenge lead to the exploration of unknown territory. Cavers seem to be drawn irresistibly towards the unknown and will develop themselves until they are at the limits of their physical and mental capability. Having reached these, they have to accept that the challenge is then to use their assets as effectively as possible. This is particularly true for the older caver as he finds limitations that themselves present new challenges in caves that in his youth were no problem. The older caver is always on a voyage into the unknown; wondering where rheumatism will strike next or where an increasing lack of suppleness will lead!

Whoever we are and whatever our abilities, the caves provide a limitless resource of unknown passages and experiences. No aerial surveys can hunt them out. The route to the unknown lies there for the finding and those who travel in the darkness can often see more with their feeble lights than those dazzled in the sunshine.

8

Water Icicle

Water Icicle.

Amiable companions to share the enjoyment of a caving trip are an essential ingredient in the best caving recipes. The chores such as tackle hauling are easier, there is more illumination on the underground scene, and in addition, the friendly conversation distracts the mind from tired limbs, and shortens tedious or arduous passages. However, it is sometimes convenient to go caving alone. Solo caving is not recommended, but experienced cavers sometimes break this rule. Knowing that the safety margins are reduced, the solo caver must always be alert and ready to deal with the unexpected.

One summer, Dilys, Catherine and I drove out to Water Icicle Close near Monyash for a family picnic. The warm breath of summer barely ruffled the trees, swallows circled high above and the cows were grazing contentedly in the warm meadows. We ate our lunch in the sunshine and lay for some time replete and sleepy in the short grass at the lane end. I had planned to visit Water Icicle Close mine which was in a field nearby, aiming to descend and ascend its entrance shaft several times to improve my physical fitness, rather like an athlete doing pressups. However, it seemed such a pleasant afternoon that I was tempted to spend it just sunbathing. Besides, I have no great affection for old mines.

Old mines are eerie places, redolent of miners' castoff clothes, stone dust and fusty roof timbers. The narrow 'coffin' levels, hewn with regular strokes of the pick and sized economically for stooping only, are slightly claustrophobic. The piles of 'deads,' or loose debris, are often perched dangerously on rotting timber and there is usually a plethora of rusty metal to cut or trip the unwary.

There are many tales of ghosts and other weird denizens reputed to haunt certain ancient mines. One wellknown tale concerns two cavers who were resting near a large flooded level in an old mine. Their lamps were dim so that they could not see the farthest reaches of what was effectively a lake, and they were surrounded by a dank and gloomy atmosphere. Suddenly, a large splash and commotion broke the silence on the far side. Some fell thing was thrashing across the water towards them. Panicstricken, they fled!

Blissfully unaware of such thoughts in my subconscious, I stirred myself and prepared for my solo descent, leaving Dilys and Catherine lazing in the sun.

The top of the Water Icicle mineshaft is fitted with a heavy iron lid attached to a length of chain to prevent it from falling accidentally down the deep shaft. I removed the lid and placed it on the grass nearby. There was a stout iron bar across the shaft top to which I tied one end of my rope before lowering the other end out of sight into the darkness below. One final check of my harness and S.R.T. gear and, sitting on the shaft lip with my legs dangling in the void, I attached my descender to the rope and then carefully lowered myself into the shaft until the rope tautened to take my full weight. The sun on my back was uncomfortably hot, so I released the descender and slid steadily down into the cool damp air of the mine.

As I descended I could see the pickaxe cuts on the shaft sides and could admire the work of the 'old men' who had hewn their way downwards in search of lead. Eventually the narrow shaft opened out into a natural chamber and I could discern the muddy floor rising to meet me. Braking hard, I made a neat landing and released my descender from the rope. Although I had only descended just over a hundred feet, the 'rack' was too hot to hold in bare hands and I kept my gloves on, though this meant fumbling more than usual.

Three passages radiated off the chamber, each leading to exploratory digs which over the years had revealed little progress. Since I had explored all the passages before and had only dropped in for exercise, I started to prepare for the ascent. Adjusting the ascenders and harnesses occupied my thoughts fully and I was oblivious to my environment, my small world restricted to the pool of light concentrated on my hands. The darkness stretched around me, full of unseen things outside my ken. At the edge of my attention I was aware of someone coming along the passage to my right. The regular crunch of footsteps and the occasional clank of metal signified a steady movement towards me. "Must be someone from the dig," I thought carelessly. And then I thought again, a sudden chill running down my spine. "Where was his rope?" "How did he get down here?" The hairs on my neck started to rise! An atavistic douche of panic surged out of my subconscious, blotting out my reason with adrenaline. Within seconds I was fifty feet up the shaft. Pausing for breath, I peered down into the gloom but could see nothing, so continued to climb steadily up into the sunlight trying to think of an explanation.

As I approached the surface I realised what it was. A herd of cows had surrounded the top of the shaft and their steady munching in regular rhythm with the occasional kick of the lid and its chain had channeled down the shaft and echoed along the tunnels below. Feeling a complete fool and thankful that no one had seen me, I climbed out on to the grass and shooed the cows away!

9

The Berks of Birks Fell

One of the greatest hazards of caving is floodwater. Many cavers have been drowned by caves flooding to the roof or by violent currents sucking them under in stormfed streamways. Some caves like Mossdale and Coolagh River Cave emanate an atmosphere of gloom and foreboding accentuated by the mud and flood debris on the ceilings. Others are more enchanting with beautiful streamways and formations but can still trap the unwary on the wrong side of a flooded passage. Birks Fell cave in Wharfedale is such a cave, with a low and floodprone entrance series leading to an extensive series of welldecorated galleries and streamways.

The cautious caver only visits floodprone caves in dry and settled weather, so, after two weeks of drought, our club trip to Birks Fell cave was well timed. Two carloads of cavers made a rendezvous at the Buckden carpark on a hot sunny day in May. I rode up with the two Tonys and Lenny, whilst Simon and Dave brought two guests from a university club. Two other members of the university club were expected to join us, but by the time that we set off for the cave entrance high on the other side of the valley, they had not arrived.

We walked up the fell in the blazing sunshine, each stripped to the waist to keep cool and our backs bent by heavy packs of caving gear. Changing into wetsuits in the unusually dry streambed made us very sticky, so it was pleasant to wriggle into the Birks Fell entrance and savour the coolness of the entrance passages. We were soon flat out in the water of a long stony crawl that in heavy rain could flood to the roof. The crawl emerged into a larger passage with a climbable pitch of about nine metres down to the streamway. Here we fixed a ladder for the return journey and continued to a low dry chamber that had a slot on the lefthand side allowing access down to the water again.

We followed the water downward through some cascades and past a couple of avens until we had to leave the stream and climb over a rock fall. Then followed the 'First Wet Bedding Cave.' This was a surprise to me as it was just a low aquatic bedding plane with a small air space, and not at all as large as I had expected. The way on was via a rift climb followed by a complex route to the 'Second Bedding Cave,' which was slightly higher than the first one with small beaches on the righthand side, but again very wet in spite of the drought. A climb up over flowstone and into a series of boulder chambers followed.

This region of the cave seemed very young with loose blocks everywhere. At one place a wide rift demanded delicate manoeuvres over and under 'The Block,' a huge chockstone with a small aperture below leading to the stream again. The passages continued with rockfalls and occasional scrambling until we reached the aptly named 'Whitehall.' Here the bright flowstone and sparkling crystalline deposits reflected the beams of our lamps in a dazzling display of beauty. Leaving time for a closer look on our return, we forged ahead to a pool and a sharp lefthand bend in the passage that eventually narrowed to a rift. At this point we had to traverse upwards and through the constricted and flaky 'Thrutch.' After the 'Thrutch' and a brief look at the next section, Lenny, Dave and I decided that we had gone far enough and that we would go back for a closer look at 'Perfection Oxbow' and other beautyspots. The others continued on into the cave.

As we were thrutching about to change direction, two other cavers arrived at high speed, anxious to pass us in their rush to the bottom. The missing university pair had arrived! With barely a word they pushed past and hurtled on to catch up with the others. We took a leisurely stroll to 'Perfection Oxbow' and then set off for the entrance, stopping occasionally to look at the beautiful formations and to admire the passageways. In spite of our sightseeing, we made steady progress, and we were soon back in the throes of the entrance series and crawling in the water again, Dave leading, then Lenny, followed by me with Lenny's Ammotin.

Splashing and clattering, someone pushed behind me anxious to overtake. It was the university pair, now racing back to the surface! Something in their manner made me slow down a bit, and when the Ammotin fell apart in the water, disgorging its carbide contents, I could feel their emotion washing around me as I scrabbled around collecting the fizzing bits and pieces. Eventually there was a passing place and I could let them through. Unfortunately they had the same effect on Lenny as on me. It was like a Jaguar stuck in a lane behind a hay-cart! Another passing place presented itself and off they motored. Lenny and I exchanged a few caustic comments and continued our leisurely exit.

On the surface it was still warm and sunny. When we arrived the speed merchants were proudly basking in the sun discussing their exploits and condescendingly watching us emerge. As we changed into dry clothes, snatches of conversation from the heroes needled our ears as they dropped names like 'The Berger' and 'The Trew.' In spite of their extreme youth they seemed to have "Done" quite a few classic systems. I began to wonder if they had ever actually seen any of them or had ever carried tackle or had ever helped rig any of them. It seemed a cheek for them to rape the cave in front of us and not offer to help detackle. Anyway, they soon disappeared downhill to the pub, leaving us in peace.

Within a few minutes of their departure, Tony Gamble arrived hot and puffing. He was, quite unusually for him, very irate. Apparently the two speedies had gone to the bottom via a laddered pitch passing the Tonys and Simon and had somehow lost contact. As the Tonys and Simon climbed back up the pitch they assumed that the two were still below them, as they had not seen them pass and so they decided to leave the ladder in position for them to derig. It was not until they reached White Hall that they met one of the other university cavers who told them that the speedy two had gone out! Tony Reynolds manfully went back to derig the pitch. Tony Gamble rushed to catch up with the culprits and give them a piece of his mind, but they were too far ahead.

Since Lenny and I had changed out of our caving gear, we set off down to Buckden for a pint, leaving the others to surface and follow us down. At the pub the culprits were sitting in the sun with their feet on the table. Lenny and I told them what had happened, and their reaction was quite surprising. Instead of being in the least apologetic, they took a very indignant line. Whatever did such yokels as us expect from these worthies—an ungrateful, insensitive couple of opportunists such as I have never met in caving before or since! I looked forward to seeing them exposed to the wrath of Tony Reynolds, not a man to mince words, and drank my beer in silence.

The expected retribution was not realised, however. In a short while a car drew up and wafted the university pair off down the valley. When the others arrived they were disappointed not to be able to vent their feelings but soon cooled down and the issue was forgotten. So flourishes iniquity. I wondered who the Berks of Birks Fell were.

10

Evensong

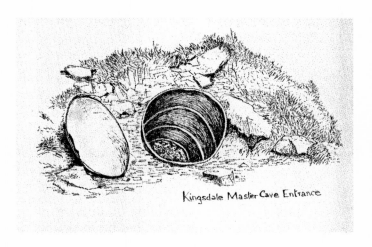

Kingsdale Master Cave Entrance

The summer sun had lost its bite and was well on its descent westwards when Lenny and I drove over the hill past Hunts Cross. We were en route from Ingleton to Kingsdale for an evening's entertainment underground. On our right, Ingleborough crouched leonine against a blue sky, its limestone pavements in a slight haze. A car glinted on the road across the dale, homeward bound for Hawes. In front of us, Kingsdale lay peaceful and serene, its grassy bottoms placid between the bleached limestone scars buttressing Gragareth and the steeply rising flanks of Whernside. We cruised downhill and along the dale, braking to rest on the verge opposite Braida Garth, the only visible habitation and alighted. Over the wall, we could see the orange lid of the valley entrance to the Kingsdale Master Cave, our ultimate destination.

Kingsdale, with its sporting and easily accessible cavities, has attracted potholers for many years. At weekends the roadside teems with their halfdressed bodies as they change clothes to enter the limestone. The early tourists used to visit Yordas, which still sports a stone-walled entrance with an arch and steps. The Yorkshire Ramblers first descended the vast maw of Rowten Pot in 1897. Simpson's, Swinsto and many of the other potholes were explored in the first half of this century, but the Master Cave linking these was not excavated until 1966.

The upper entrances to the West Kingsdale cave system all lie close to the green Turbary road, an old peatcutter's track running from Hunts Cross to Yordas Wood and now a scenic promenade for walkers and cavers. Lenny and I planned to climb up to the Turbary Road, enter Swinsto, rappel down the intervening shafts and potholes to the Master Cave and emerge from the Valley Entrance before the pubs closed—an exhilarating, sporting and refreshingly aqueous descent that we had both been anticipating through the hot summer's day.

Changing at the roadside like countless others before us, we pulled on our wetsuits, donned our helmets, fitted our electric lamps and buckled up our climbing harnesses in preparation for our trip underground. We sorted out the rest of the tackle, two 120-ft. ropes, descenders and spare slings, and locked up the car. At the weekend, we would probably have used only one rope, on the certainty that if it became stuck on rappel, another party would soon be through to release it. Tonight we hoped to have the system to ourselves and considered the extra rope well worth the trouble. Shouldering our gear, we set off up the steep track leading to the Turbary Road and soon began to perspire in our clinging wetsuits.

Pausing by the crags to rest our legs and lungs, we gazed at the tranquil scene around us. Nothing stirred except for the rooks and the imperceptibly cropping sheep. A curlew called, answering the echoing bleat of a lamb. Nearby, a bumblebee hummed about its busy way in the bracken. The scent of crushed grass sweetened the air and mixed with the earthy tang of the limestone. The light had an orange tint by now and the colours of the dale looked soft and mellow. We stood, timeless, entranced, forgetting our purpose and ourselves—overcome by Nature's assault on our senses. Above us, a sheep dislodged a stone. Rattling down the slope, it broke the spell and we commenced the upward climb. Soon we were on the Turbary Road and then searching beyond for the inconspicuous manhole of the Swinsto entrance, hidden amongst the grassy hummocks and shakeholes.

Once located, the Swinsto entrance is quite distinctive; a well-defined hole with a small flat-bottomed stream running along underneath, like a storm drain. We turned our lamps on, adjusted our gear and, Lenny entering first, we inserted ourselves into the hole, twisting to fit our bodies to the riftlike crawl that followed. The first pitch was not far and its noise was alluring. At the top, the passage was too narrow for us to stand abreast, so whilst Lenny uncoiled his rope, I fixed a sling to a convenient rock further back from the lip. One end of the rope was then threaded through the sling and pulled through so that the rope hung doubled down the pitch, which was only about twenty feet deep, although making a lot of noise about it. Attaching his descender, Lenny tested his weight on the rope and then jumped outwards and down the pitch, spray flying everywhere and sparkling in the beam of his lamp. A shout from below and I too slid rapidly down, flying through the spray effortlessly to splash to rest at the bottom.

We now had to recover the rope for use on the following pitches. A sharp tug on one of the ends and down it came, swishing and slithering into a heap at my feet. The shaft loomed above us, water gushing out against its leaden walls, the thin white threads of our connection to the surface gone. We were now totally committed to the descent.

Lenny coiled up the rope and replaced it on his shoulder. The small chamber below the fall had two ways off and we entered the downstream exit, about a yard high, the start of the notorious Swinsto Long

Crawl. Before us was a crawl in the water over rough rock and pebbles for about a thousand feet. Knowing what we had to endure, we set a steady pace, glad of the protection afforded by our wetsuits.

In the old days when we used ladder and wetsuits were not invented, the crawl was very arduous, particularly as at that time there was no way out at the bottom and the crawl had to be negotiated again on the return journey. At some places the crawl was flat out, at others the stones were painful on knees and forearms. I remember that we discussed ocean-going yachts as we crawled. Lenny possessed a yachtmaster's ticket and was an experienced yachtsman. Lounging in the water on one of our numerous rests, we discussed navigation, winds, tides and the West Coast of Scotland, oblivious to the low roof and contortions of the crawl. In this way the time passed quickly and soon we were able to rise to a stoop. The water began to flow more quickly and the distant roar of a waterfall could be heard. We gathered speed and it was not long before we were at the next pitch, about twenty feet deep, with a splendid waterfall into a dark pool below.

We rappelled off a rock belay on a doubled rope, hurtling through the water to aim for a submerged ledge, just visible under the pool surface. The unwary caver risks a ducking here, as we knew from a previous trip when a hydrophilic friend dropped into the pool on purpose to make a big splash and went right under. Stepping across to the other side, we recovered the rope, which plummeted down dutifully into the pool to make coiling easy. This time, however, we each took one end and made separate coils, continuing until we had a few feet of slack between us and a fifty foot coil apiece.

The next pitch was only a short distance away and a large cylindrical beam was jammed across the top for a belay point. Lenny threw his coil over the top of the beam. I lobbed mine underneath and the pitch was rigged. So we made another refreshing descent through the water, both of us getting into the swing of things. We seemed to be caught in the downward rush of the stream, surging on, the walls and spume aglitter from our lamps, the cave itself seemingly alive around us. This was the entertainment that we sought, free and exciting. At the bottom, we pulled the rope down easily from the slippery wooden beam and made up two coils as before. We now had further to go, and clambered over the rock linked together like cars on tow. At the top of the next waterfall, there was an eyehole in the rock, slimy with moonmilk on flowstone.

One coil through the hole, the other down the pitch and we were off again, to land thirty feet below in a sizeable chamber with a shallow pool. The rope retrieved easily and we were ready for the 'Big' pitch following.

The 'Big' pitch was actually split into two sections by a large ledge about sixty feet down, so our doubled rope was just long enough. A large shackle was bolted to the lefthand wall at the top, not really in the best position for rappelling, but very secure. We fed one coil of the rope through and dropped the other down the slope. I clipped my descender into the doubled strands now hanging into space. Leaning out, I peered at the ledge below, using the beam of my lamp to try and see if the rope was long enough. Satisfied, I jumped outwards and let the descender drop me down. I swung like a pendulum bob back into the water and spray; out again, dropping down in a series of jumps until I landed on the spray-lashed ledge with just enough rope to brake with. I unclipped and pulled one of the rope ends gently to test that it would slip through the shackle above. It seemed free, so I shouted up to Lenny and moved back out of the spray.

On a previous trip, I had failed to realise that the rope that I was using had thick plastic ferrules on both ends instead of on one end only. Noticing that one end had a ferrule with the length and club number on it, I pulled on that end to retrieve the rope from the shackle, erroneously thinking that the other end was without a ferrule. Unfortunately there was and it jammed as the rope end passed into the shackle at the top of the pitch. I was unable to dislodge the rope and had to leave it and continue on the spare. Luckily, a party following behind brought it out for me, saving a return journey. To some extent, rappelling underground is always a calculated risk and one should take all precautions to avoid getting stuck unnecessarily.

Lenny hurtled down to join me on the ledge, the rope humming with his descent. Carefully checking that the rope had no kinks in it and that there was only one ferrule, we pulled at the ferruled end. The rope moved steadily, but we pulled harder to speed it up and with a perceptible jerk, the free end passed through the shackle, allowing the remainder to drop down. What a relief!

We were now standing on a windswept ledge, battered by the incessant rain from the waterfall above. The limestone here had a yellowish appearance in the glow from our lamps that seemed to dispel some of the chill that soon became apparent. In the days of woolens and 'Long Johns,' the risk of exposure from the icy water and the draught made this a particularly arduous expedition and even in wetsuits, we did not feel inclined to linger.

The ledge tapered off along the lip of the next vertical drop, to a point where it was possible to lean out and reach a hanger bolted to the wall opposite. This belay was festooned with slings in various states of decay left by previous cavers. We decided to fit our own attachment and soon had a short length of rope threaded through the hanger and knotted into a loop to take the main rappel rope. These manoeuvres, performed precariously over the void below, were soon completed and we rappelled down avoiding most of the water to land in a large chamber.

The rope was easily recovered again and coiled up, as the next pitch was some way off down a steeply descending passage. The stream sped onwards past smooth and curving walls. We could now sense the subconscious pull of the unseen mastercave beyond. We soon warmed up with the downward business of our descent, crossing occasional small pools and swarming down several short climbs and rapids. At one point, the water entered a crack and we took a dry route to a natural flight of steps, then along a sloping flake of rock with a pond, on the lefthand side of the defile. A flaky protrusion was a convenient belay for the final drop into Spout Chamber twenty feet below. A rather clumsy rappel and we were wading about in the pool that filled most of the chamber, collecting up the rope. The spout was living up to its name, shooting out of a slot, to the right of the pitch that we had just descended and crashing down into the pool in a parabolic arc like a gigantic firehose. The power and velocity of the water was very obvious and we were glad that our route had avoided the issue here.

From Spout Chamber, the route became more constricted, although the smoothness of the walls made progress easy. In some places we had to slide between the rock sideways, in others slip down to an occasional crawl past a constriction. This part of the cave always seems more homely now an easy way out at the bottom exists, the rocks enfolding the caver rather than resisting his passage. In the past, I always felt it to be inimical and menacing; the pitches to the surface were far behind and the tumble of boulders below most unwelcoming.

Eventually we emerged into a large passage with droplets of water floating down from an aven in the roof and with huge blocks littering the floor. The descent became less steep as we were nearing the bottom of the cave. The roof rose even higher and soon we reached a cubby-hole in the lefthand wall where the eighty-foot shaft of Slit pot drops down from the Simpson's system. Lenny pointed out the 'Great Aven' pitch, which he had rappelled down recently as an easier alternative, although it was about 130 ft. deep. We discussed the possibility of a future trip 'en rappel' down this route from Simpson's and shone our lights up into the roof probing for the inlet hole before continuing downstream.

The passage ahead was high and wide, with several blocks jammed across the streamway and quickly led us to the last pitch. Although this pitch is freeclimbable, we did not relish the idea of a downward climb in the water on the shattered looking holds and so we rappelled off a recently planted bolt belay, into the final chamber of Swinsto.

In my early visits years ago, this was the end of the cave and after a desultory poke among the boulders covering the floor, we would have a snack and set off on the tiring haul to the surface. Since then, more determined cavers had cleared a route through the boulder choke and discovered the master cave beyond. The way on was now obvious on our right—a hole in the boulder ruckle. Taking care not to disturb any loose rocks, we dropped down the hole and lowered ourselves into a low crawl passing after a short distance through pools of icy cold water. Crawling on gravel and pebbles, with the odd sandbank, we pressed on to reach dry land as quickly as possible. After the rapid flight down the airy pitches above it seemed very anticlimatic and mundane progress. However, it was not long before we were able to stand up from the confines of the crawls and step out into the Kingsdale Master cave.

The atmosphere in the master cave was fresh and invigorating after the foggy bedding planes, and puddles of the Swinsto connection. The noise and chatter of the water flowing from the Rowten sumps on our left seemed to contain human voices, high and tinkling. We felt a tinge of envy at the discoverers and could imagine their excitement at finding such a superb streamway now confronting us. The way on downstream was wide and high, with clean sculptured walls glittering from the reflected beams of our lights and several water chutes running in a smooth streambed. We made rapid progress and, rounding a corner, soon came to the downstream sump, scene of the epic dives through to Keld Head. On the left and about thirty feet above us, we could see the Roof Tunnel connection to the surface.

At weekends, descending trippers would ladder this pitch, but tonight we would have to climb up to it on the righthand wall. Lenny climbed first, being the better climber and lifelined me up second. We traversed over a rock bridge and into the dry tunnel. Stooping and occasionally wriggling past obstructions, we quickly reached the last obstacle, The Valley Entrance Duck. The duck was low down under the lefthand wall of a small chamber containing a waist deep pool. The roof of the duck was smooth and rounded, yellowish in colour, with about six inches of airspace. Heads on one side to keep our nostrils out of the water, we slipped slowly through, careful not to create waves that could engulf us and stood up in a small chamber on the other side. Water gushing from the holes in our wetsuits, we squelched into the final chamber, admiring the white encrustations on its walls.

We could smell the surface now and one more gravelly crawl along a tubelike passage led to the oil drum entrance, its interior polished by the passage of many bodies. The lid was on, so I gave it a push and it fell outside with a clatter. The evening stars twinkled through the hole inviting us out into the dusk. We squirmed out, refitted the lid and in the twilight, walked back to the waiting car.

The air smelt sweet and heady after the cave and the evening air seemed remarkably warm. Lenny recovered the car key from its hiding place and unlocked the boot. We peeled off our wetsuits, towelled ourselves dry and pulled on our surface clothes. The wet gear was soon loaded and after a quick look around to check that nothing was left on the ground, we sank into the car seats and drove off into the falling night.

Whilst Kingsdale slumbered, we slaked our thirsts with foaming pints, refreshed and cleansed in spite of the mud behind our ears!

11

Gaping Ghyll Main Shaft

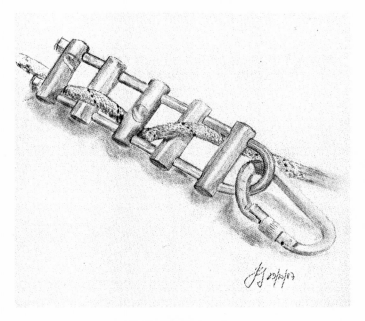

A 'rack' descender

The image of Gaping Ghyll to most Dalesfolk is a pothole on the fells near Ingleborough Hill. To the fellwalker, it is an interesting detour on the path to the summit. To the tourist venturing above the 'handbag line' of Trow Gill on a Bank Holiday, it represents a pound's worth of excitement plummeting into the underworld on a winch, or the turning point for home. To the potholer, Gaping Ghyll is a vast system of

underground passages with many surface connections, the most spectacular being the Main Shaft, one hundred and ten metres deep, that
swallows Fell Beck after its run off Ingleborough.

The waters of Fell Beck flow through the system to emerge at Ingleborough Cave over a mile distant from the point of engulfment. For
many years, potholers sought the connecting passages without success,
discovering many miles of passages in the process and eventually forcing a connection. The furthest reaches have names evoking feelings of
distance and remoteness such as 'Far Country' and 'Far Waters.' A visit
to these places is a serious undertaking. However, for the practitioners
of the recently developed 'Static rope technique' or SRT, the Main
Shaft itself is a magnet.

Early one sunny morning in July, a carload of cavers from our club
in the Potteries set off up the M6 to rendezvous in Clapham village car
park with two others living in the area. We planned to descend Main
Shaft Gaping Ghyll on a static rope, returning the same way after a
brief underground exploration.

On our arrival, a sudden downpour broke the promise of the early
morning sunshine. Clapham car park soon lay gloomily inert under a
cloud, puddles erupting from the deluge. We sat in our cars wondering
if our plans would have to be changed. Ralph, our club secretary, sat
polishing his glasses and sucking his beard pensively. Tony Gamble,
one of our static rope experts, soft-spoken and laconic, gazed out at the
rain, occasionally responding to the animated talk of Tony Reynolds,
our club hard man. Lenny, the fifth member of our team, had not yet
arrived. Late as usual, his car splashed up alongside and his cheery voice
broke my reverie. We decided to sit it out.

At last there was a gap in the clouds and the sun appeared, somewhat ashamedly. There was nothing for it but to change into our
waterproof overalls, pull on our boots, hoist our packs and ropes on to
our shoulders and set off up the village en route for Gaping Ghyll.
Each of us had his personal climbing gear, 'Rappel Racks' to attach to
the rope for the descent and various ascending devices—'Jumars,'

'Jammers,' 'Ropewalkers' and 'Poignées'—to name but a few. Although our loads were lighter than in the days of ladder technique, they still seemed surprisingly heavy.

Sunshine and showers punctuated the walk up the 'Nature Trail' in Ingleborough Park, through Trow Gill and on to the moor. Our loads seemed to become heavier and our blood pulsed hot with the effort of the climb, so that by the time that we eventually reached Gaping Ghyll, we all felt like having a rest and a cool pint. However, there was work to be done. We had to construct a dam across Fell Beck to divert the water from its well worn route where it was cascading noisily into the Main Shaft of Gaping Ghyll. Luckily for us, the beck was not in flood in spite of the recent showers. Shifting boulders, pieces of turf, polythene sacks and pebbles, we soon had most of the water flowing down the aptly named 'Rathole,' an alternative route into the system on one side of the beck. The leakage from this dam was easily diverted into another hole further along. After about an hour of hard navvying, we managed to stop the flow of water into the Main Shaft. With luck the dams would be strong enough to cope with any further showers.

After a hasty snack for ballast, we prepared for the descent, struggling into our climbing harnesses, clipping on our various climbing devices and donning helmets and lamps. Tony Gamble was the first to be changed and ready, so he set off to rig the first pitch.

Sunk into the moor, on the side opposite Fell Beck, was an ancient wooden stake. Tony inspected this dubiously, pulling it sideways to test its strength. Satisfied, he tied one end of the rope to the stake and threw the rest into the shaft. The rope hummed as it fell, the noise magnified by the enormous windpipe of the open shaft. Connecting himself to the rope, Tony tried his weight on the stake once more and descended the grassy slope below to land on a small ledge. Here there was a bolt driven into the rock, to which he attached the rope. This would give additional security and ease any fears about the ancient stake. He abseiled down to the very lip of the Main Shaft and hung there looking for a way of preventing the rope from rubbing on the rocky ledge. Here there was another bolt to attach the rope to, but it looked rather rusty, even though it was ideally placed for the next leg of the descent. After some thought, he clipped the rope into this, changed over on to the rope hanging freely in the shaft and calmly slid off into the abyss.

The rest of us, who had been discussing the rain, the state of the dams, our aches and pains and whether it was a good day for doing Gaping Ghyll, watched all this with mixed feelings. Who was going to go next? Hoisting a wellworn rope to his shoulder, Tony Reynolds decided it was his turn and walked around the moor to the stake. He clipped himself into the fixed rope and we heard a faint shout float up from below. He gently lowered himself down to the small ledge, crossed the bolt and descended to the lip. Here, he spent some time transferring his weight on to the main pitch rope and then he too slid out of sight.

Ralph and I looked at each other and again at the dams. Lenny, his arm stiff from a TAB jab, fiddled about adjusting his harnesses. Ralph waded out to fix a small leak that had developed in the main dam, so I was next! I walked over to the stake and listened. I could hear various noises coming up the shaft but they sounded unintelligible. The main rope looked slack, so I checked my gear for the last time clipped my descender into the top rope, worked my way down to the first ledge and then abseiled down to the lip.

Looking down from my precarious position, the view was impressive. The shaft yawned below me, smooth and curved, with a dull chocolatebrown appearance, glistening and precipitous. Far below, the red overalls of the two Tonys gleamed brightly. They appeared as small specks against the pale grey of Birkbeck's ledge on which they were standing. What a drop! Through a slight fog, I could see the waiting floor of the Main Chamber even further below. With some difficulty, I transferred my weight to the main rope, manoeuvring past the rusty bolt, the void below me sucking at every movement. Loosening the descender, I started it sliding down the rope at a steady rate, using both hands on the free rope to control my descent. Almost like a bird, I began to fly down the shaft, past the mossy patches at the top and on down into the moist gullet of Gaping Ghyll.

Zooming down close to the polished limestone walls, on a superb ride, I braked to rest on Birkbeck's ledge. A flying sheep was lying in a puddle, its entrails pink and yellow and its eyes glazed pale blue like the sky from which it came. Oddly enough, it did not smell in spite of being quite dead. Looking up through the vast shaft, I could see an oval of bright sky fringed with grass or heather. The rope seemed to disappear upwards almost to a vanishing point like a strand of hair.

John Birkbeck was the first man to land on this ledge, in 1842, but went no further. This was my first visit too, but perhaps less daunting. The ledge seemed quite roomy and relatively dry, in spite of the spray from the lateral shaft nearby where the water was now falling due to the diversion above. The walls were slightly undercut and at one place overhanging enough to give some protection from possible stonefalls. The way on was outwards over a short slope which ended in blackness about thirty feet further down, where Tony Gamble was hammering in a bolt to anchor the rope and prevent it from rubbing. Tony Reynolds, belayed to a bolt in the wall of the ledge, sat waiting. We chatted above the noise of the falling water and the hammering from below. It could have been the companionship and the security of good ropes, but the ledge seemed a pleasant place. It would certainly be a veritable haven on the way back up.

The hammering stopped. A shouted conversation ensued and Tony G. set off for the bottom. Soon his light appeared far below and away from the pitch, moving into the Main Chamber. There were no signs of Ralph or Lenny arriving and no response to our rude shouts up the shaft, so Tony R. set off too. He soon slithered down the slope, passed the newly positioned bolt and disappeared from sight and sound. The ledge still had a friendly aura although I was quite alone. I felt near to the rock and very close to Nature; such moments are the true refreshment of all outdoor folk.

Noises from above disturbed my contemplation and silhouetted against the sky, I could see someone, probably Lenny, by his bulk, struggling to cross the bolt at the top. Two lights were visible below now, so it was time for me to leave. I clipped my descender into the lower rope and gingerly negotiated the slope. Under a deluge of water and spray, I transferred to the last section of rope, in midair, high above the Main Chamber. Releasing the tension on the descender I dropped smoothly down past a wall of rock flakes and out into the blackness. My light seemed to go out, its beam lost in the surrounding void. What a sensation! I could not resist a whoop or two and a bit more speed. I dropped almost in free fall, braking fiercely as the floor rushed up out of gloom, to land clattering on the cobbles of the Main Chamber.

Unclipping myself from the rope, I turned and walked over to the others, still sheltering from the falling spray. Overhead, the waterfall rattled continuously, sparkling in the daylight filtering down the shaft. I could see Lenny coming over the slope on the last leg of his descent and soon he was flying down to join us. We gathered around him to find out what had delayed him. Apparently the dams were giving trouble and after fixing them, Ralph had decided to stay behind and keep a weather eye on them. At least we could be certain that our return up the shaft would not be prevented by the heavily descending contents of Fell Beck.

Shining the powerful beams of our electric headlamps to find the route, we located the exit from the Main Chamber and made our way to the connection with Bar Pot, another entrance to the system much frequented by ladder enthusiasts. Stooping in the low passages, we were soon at the foot of the last pitch of this route, but there were no signs of activity, so we set off back to explore the Main Chamber. This was the first time that I had visited Main Chamber for at least a decade and even though my eyes were by now accustomed to the darkness, it still seemed smaller than it used to be. Perhaps it had grown in my imagination in the intervening years. We strolled down the 'West End,' had a desultory look around and then walked back to the waiting rope.

Since I was the oldest and least fit, I started up first, intending to have a good rest on Birkbeck's ledge. The pitch seemed deceptively long and I bounced about on the rope, which seemed more elastic than usual, pushing on my ascenders that were attached to my chest harness and footloops. I seemed to have been hard at it for ages and yet the top of the pitch looked as distant as ever. I rested in my harness and looked down. The floor looked quite far below and I felt comforted at the hard-won progress. I pushed on, trying to achieve a steady rhythm, but frustrated in this attempt by the bouncy rope.

After a while, I reached the flaky rock wall and because there was now less rope above, stopped bouncing and made rapid progress. Hot and panting with the exertion, I arrived at the bolt. As I manoeuvred across to the upper section of rope, the falling spray cooled me, the water running down my sleeves and face. I inched my way up the slope towards Birkbeck's ledge. Eventually I gained the ledge and was able to signal to the others that the rope was clear.

I moved underneath the small overhang, heaped the loose coils of the slack in the top rope to make a cushion and sat down, tingling with the luxury. Pulling off my helmet, I extracted a bar of chocolate from the lining and sat at ease idly contemplating the dead sheep, munching for energy. I peered upwards into the light considering the rest of the climb to the surface.

A clinking noise of metal on rock sounded from below and Lenny appeared puffing and grunting as he scrambled up the slope. He too had found the lower pitch deceptively tiring. The next pitch looked at least as hard, but it was on new rope. I shared out the rest of the chocolate, pulled the top rope into my ascenders and in a fit of enthusiasm started the climb upwards.

For the first few feet the rope swung me against the wall, but soon I was hanging freely in space and managing to climb in a smooth rhythm. Push up the 'Poignée,' push up with the legs, push up the

'Poignée', and push up with the legs. The clicking of the ascenders became regular like an old grandfather clock. Breath, legs, arms, movement in unison. The rope slid smoothly through the ascenders without bouncing, seeming to aid my upward surge with its shining newness. About three quarters of the way up, I paused to look down and could see that one of the others had joined Lenny on the ledge. I pushed on upwards into the mossy zone near the top. Looking down at me from above, precariously leaning out over the edge, was a female fellwalker. She obviously had no conception of the size of the drop below her so I shouted for her to take care and she withdrew.

A few more movements and I arrived at the bolt on the lip. Hot and sweating, I paused to regain my breath and rest my arms for the next manoeuvre. I twisted around and shouted across to Ralph, patiently guarding the dams. Nearby, sitting on the rocks like a theatre audience, was a group of fellwalkers. I do not know what they expected to see, but I took plenty of care crossing the bolts above and scrambling across the grass. I was up!

Unclipping from the rope, I loosened my harness and walked around the edge of the shaft to Ralph, feeling pleasantly tired and mildly exhilarated. He produced a bottle of barley water from his rucksack and offered me some. It was just what I needed and I slaked my thirst swilling the cool liquid around inside my mouth like a wine taster with a noble claret. We walked back to the edge to watch Lenny ascending. Soon he too was back on Terra Firma sipping the barley water, his TAB-jabbed arm swollen and throbbing from the climb. The two Tonys as fit as ever, took very little time to surface and were soon busy pulling up the ropes. We pulled the dams apart and released Fell Beck to its old course, hurtling down Main Shaft to crash on Birkbeck's ledge in a hurricane of spray. Just as we were tidying up and checking that everything was as we had found it, the heavens opened in another downpour. We hastily lifted our packs to our shoulders and heads bowed into the driving rain, scurried off across the moor en route for Clapham. Gaping Ghyll roared a farewell, and settled down to its eternal drinking once again.

Our intrusion was over.

12

Pilgrimage to the Pierre St Martin

Salle Loubens

A knock on the door at 5 a.m. Time to get up! I whispered that I was awake and quietly got out of bed, feeling for my clothes in the darkness to avoid waking Dilys. Holidaying on the Côte Basque at Bidart meant an early start for a day's caving in the Pyrenees. Today we were off to the Pierre St. Martin, one of the deepest caves in the world. For me, it would also be a pilgrimage to the resting-place of Marcel Loubens, tragically killed in the early explorations—a catastrophic event still clearly remembered from my early caving years.

I crept downstairs to join Trevor outside at the car, packed the night before and we drove off into the morning. Our rendezvous was the French caving hut at St. Pierre d'Irube near Bayonne. At the club-house, the lights were on and Gilbert, with his young nephew Didier, was busy sorting out tackle for the trip. Gilbert suggested that we went in his car, as he knew the route well. We crammed our gear into the boot and ourselves into the seats. Gilbert locked up the clubhouse, strapped himself into the driving seat, started the engine and with a squeal of tyres set off for St. Engrâçe.

Motoring steadily on the quiet morning roads, we travelled via Pey-rehorade and Sauveterre to Mauleon, an ancient town with a good bakery. Gilbert stopped to buy croissants and baguettes and then we were off again, the sweet aroma of freshly baked bread filling our nos-trils. As we swung through the lanes in amongst the summer maize, we breakfasted on the croissants, two apiece, sweet and flaky. Soon the scenery became more wooded and limestone outcrops could be seen. Some had names like 'The Gendarmes Hat,' others were innominate but grand nevertheless. We passed the impressive Kakoueta gorge and continued to climb up past a hydroelectric scheme to the small village of St. Engrâçe. In a flurry of dust and hurtling chickens, we pulled up outside the sturdy village church.

Easing ourselves from the car, we stretched our cramped limbs in the cold mountain air. It was 8.30 a.m. Pulling on jumpers against the chill, we walked over to the village bar and ordered coffee. Sipping the brew, hot, black and acrid, we waited for Michel, president of the Departmental Caving Group who was collecting the key to the E.D.F. tunnel, our point of entry into the Pierre St. Martin. Like Gilbert, he was an old friend of many caving trips and a member of the local club—Ziloko Gizonak *(The Basque for Cave man)*. When he eventually arrived we had lots to talk about, especially as it was the first time we had seen him for a year. Now, however, for the march!

We drove downhill through the village to park at the roadside just before a bridge over a small stream. As we loaded our caving tackle into our rucksacks, I hoped that my photographic gear would repay its weight. The Frenchmen seemed to travel very light and Trevor and I seemed overloaded by comparison. A last check around and the march began. Crossing the stream further along near a small farmstead, we flexed our leg muscles up a steep rocky path in amongst the gorse, now crackling in the sun. As we climbed, the sun seemed to become hotter, so we were very glad to turn on to a bridletrack under trees. After about half an hour of walking, we reached the Ravine d'Arphidia and the path became steeper. Trevor and I started to fall behind, heavily loaded and unfit from too many days on the beaches and in tempting restaurants. Luckily the others found a bed of wild strawberries and we caught them up whilst they were still grazing. Crimson, juicy and abundant, the fruit was irresistible and, having eaten our fill, we ground back into action again. Soon we could see the compressed air pipe used to drill the EDF tunnel and were told it was not much further. Eventually, hot and sweaty, we toiled up the last steep climb and grounded our loads outside the ramshackle hut by the tunnel entrance.

Sitting outside in the sunshine, we quenched our thirsts and tucked into pâté and baguette, a superb view feasting our eyes. Such sunny clear weather in these parts was rare and it seemed unreal to think that our needs were underground in a black humidity. Replete, we adjourned to the hut obviously well frequented, from the litter and graffiti on the walls. Using the large survey on the back wall of the hut, Michel outlined our proposed route in the cave. We would enter by the EDF tunnel and passing through the enormous chamber of La Verna, go upstream to the Lepineux shaft and then return by the same route, perhaps taking a look at the Gouffre Arphidia on the way out. It seemed a pleasing prospect and I hoped that I had enough flashbulbs to take pictures in the vast chambers and galleries.

Swatting the voracious '*taons*,' or horseflies, which were relishing our blood as a change of diet, we changed into our caving gear. Michel put his helmet on. He had walked up clad only in a light boiler suit that he intended to wear underground. Obviously it was going to be a dry trip! Trevor pulled on a wetsuit and I 'Damarts' and a polyurethane boilersuit. I suspected that I would be better off in shorts *á la South Wales*. My ammo tin of photographic gear was topped up with chocolate and Kendal mint-cake. I took a last swig of the Vittel and we were ready to go.

As we approached the steel doors of the tunnel, we could hear the noise of the wind whistling out through the cracks. When Michel unloosed the catch, the doors flew apart with the pressure of the cold air inside and blew out the flame on his acetylene lamp. I led the way in, my electric lamp throwing a sharp beam. The extravagant size of the artificial tunnel was amazing. Michel propped the doors open for our return. The tunnel continued to another set of doors, again with a tremendous air pressure behind them. Keeping right at the various junctions, in some places passing beneath rotting timbers supporting the more shattered parts of the roof, we carried on. After about 300 metres, we suddenly emerged into the unimaginable blackness of La Verna.

La Verna is the largest underground chamber that I have ever seen—a shock to the senses like free space without stars, or like the open fells on a starless night. To attempt a better view, we walked up onto a promontory where a *'Tyrolienne'* was rigged to the far side. Although I could pick out the roof with my powerful beam and see the waterfalls and floor below, I could not see the far extremities. We seemed to be floating in a vast blackness, the waterfall noise echoing faintly around us. I had still not obtained my bearings when we set off up a path traversing to the left of the chamber. Apparently we could not descend to the bottom to avoid disturbing a colony of rare insects there. The route led in amongst the boulders, with a rope descent at one point and eventually we scrambled down to stream level. Hopping from rock to rock, we crossed over the stream and started to climb a huge boulder pile on the other side. It was just like fell walking, the cavern was so enormous. Soon the sweat was dripping down my face with the exertion of climbing and scrambling. I envied Michel with his lighter clothing, calmly forging ahead in unencumbered coolness.

At the end of La Verna, the route merged into the enormous Salle Chevalier. Once again we clambered over the fells, keeping the stream on our right, occasionally scaling huge blocks the size of houses, with pauses to search out the best route. The place was so huge that our lights gave us little impression of the whole cavern and we scrambled on in a local pool of light until we reached a small lake, deep, blue and icy cold. There was a narrow ledge on the righthand side facing upstream that we climbed around to avoid a wetting. A low bedding plane led onward through a boulder ruckle and up to the Salle Adelie, a smaller yet still enormous cavern. The route here was high upon the righthand wall, with a traverse at one point along a knifelike ledge with a fixed handline. After some distance we entered the Salle Queffelec, where the red mud cast a warmth, but dulled our beams and slowed our progress. The next obstacle was a 20-metre rope pitch down into the start of the 'Metro,' a large well decorated gallery about 30 metres high. Adjectives for size are relative. In the Pierre St. Martin this place only rated a 'large' as it was one of the smaller sections and probably the only suitable site for photography with my limited flash capability. The gour pools at the far end were clear and azure with crystal barriers like delicate cake icing, and potential photographic subjects for the return journey. The Metro ended in a boulder pile with a slot over near the lefthand wall. Gilbert wriggled through and shouted for us to follow. The route led up into the Salle Loubens, dry and silent, the water passing underneath somewhere. We did a complete circuit of this chamber before finding the way out through a vertical rift at the far end. A sandy passage followed past a hole down through jagged rocks to a small stream off route to the right. Climbing ever upwards, steeply in some sections, we emerged into the Salle Elizabeth Casteret. The route out of here took some finding, as it was high up at the crest of a steep slope beneath an enormous boulder choke. A fixed rope was in position for the climb up into the Lepineux Chamber. The climb completed, a few more rocks surmounted and we were able to walk over to the boulder pile where Loubens, one of the early explorers, was laid to rest after his fatal fall in 1952.

Here, deep below the earth, there was an aura of calm, cool and eternal. The scene of tragic events past and deep emotions long spent was now empty like the discarded shell of a chrysalis. The sooty inscription was still legible: *"Içi Marcel Loubens a vécu les dernières jours de sa vie courageuse."* Our pilgrimage was over!

Leaving our gear, we struggled up the rubble cone under the Lepineux shaft, small boulders and pebbles rattling down the scree slope behind us. I arrived at the summit, thigh muscles straining from the constant slipping and slithering of the ascent. My beam illuminated the fissure of the shaft in the ceiling high above. It was smaller than I had imagined from the accounts I had read of the early explorations and the twists in it allowed no daylight to penetrate. Sparkling and twinkling, a fine spray of water droplets rained down—a potential torrent in bad weather. We peered into the blackness around us, just like the early explorers must have done, imagining their feelings in the vastness and depth. The tumbled blocks and gigantic roof falls signified a cave in its youth, alive, active and dangerous. Poised on top of the rubble cone, we were at the end of our trip, but for the discoverers it had been a magnificent beginning.

Scree-running down the cone, we returned to our gear. Whilst I unpacked my camera, the others unpacked their food. Michel had some interesting dried bananas, Gilbert *saucisson*, Didier raisins, and Trevor, mintcake. As we chatted and ate, the atmosphere was dispelled. However, we were a temporary phenomenon and the cave, timeless, awaited our departure. I took some photographs and we left.

The return journey was rapid and relatively easy. On the way in, we had climbed a considerable height and now it was mostly downhill. At the stream just before the Salle Loubens we stopped for a drink, crystal clear, cold and refreshing. The acetylene lamps were recharged with water also. Further on, in the Metro, I photographed the bluegreen gour pools, the flowstone formations and the beautiful vista of the streamway. The flashbulbs threw large pools of light into the vastness. We continued on our way through the huge chambers, sometimes taking a different route from that on the way in to look at items of interest or merely by default. After a surprisingly short time, we arrived back at La Verna. Entering from the Salle Chevalier, La Verna was less of a shock to the senses, but indescribably vast nevertheless. Our pupils, widened by several hours in darkness, gave greater vision and we had a better perspective. The route down to the stream and through the boulders to the E.D.F. tunnel seemed to take a long time however, with numerous forgotten obstacles in the way. On the promontory again, I tried to illuminate the Aranzadi Wall opposite but the distance and the moist atmosphere dissipated my beam. One last look around and we reentered the tunnel, its entrance easily missed in the vast cavern.

On the way out to the surface, we detoured to visit the Gouffre d'Arphidia, a narrow rift system providing hours of arduous caving, both down in search of greater depth and upwards to connect with the Pierre St. Martin one day perhaps. Perched in the rift, we discussed the latest progress, but decided to defer a more detailed examination to some later date. Setting off again, we soon reached the inner doors and walked towards the light, the scent of the outside air heady and pungent in our nostrils. We emerged into a cloudy day, the sun sheathed to ease our walk back down.

As we changed at the hut, some other cavers arrived and we chatted until Michel reminded us of the time…He had an appointment to keep in Mauleon. Hoisting our rucksacks onto our backs, we moved off down the hill, hurrying to keep up with Michel who set a cracking pace and kept taking precipitous shortcuts through the bushes and brambles. Soon we were all back at the cars and in no time at all, loaded up and aboard. We drove up to St. Engrâçe for a beer or two and to plan our next trip of the holiday. After some discussion we decided on a visit to Betchanka and then Michel had to leave. We drank just one more beer each and then we too hit the road, Gilbert driving as steadily as ever.

The journey back seemed to pass very quickly. Trevor and I dozed a while and Didier slept all the way. We were soon in the evening glow of the lights of Bayonne. The transfer of gear to Trevor's car completed, we said our good-byes and within half an hour we were back at Bidart. Our wives, sunburnt from a day on the beach with the children asleep in bed, welcomed us home.

We sat down in the lounge with glasses of Armagnac, fruity and golden, recounting our adventures. The day had passed quickly and eventfully, but we had a distillate in our minds, warmed by the spirits that we were sipping. The memories of such days are to be nurtured, treasures for old age. It seemed fitting to close the day on the warmth and bouquet of Armagnac. And so to bed!

13

One to Two

The caver's dream of wading in a spectacular underground streamway, clean scalloped and airy, with clear water swirling live around his legs, the noise of the torrent reverberating in lofty passageways, is realised in the magnificent Nant Newydd in South Wales. This exhilarating and beautiful streamway is the main artery of Ogof Ffynnon Ddu, one of the longest and deepest cave systems in the British Isles. The underground traverse from the lower entrance, discovered in 1946, to the 'Top' entrance excavated twenty years later, can give three or four hours of subterranean pleasure and excitement that ranks high with cavers from all over the world. An added luxury is the nearby hostel of the South Wales Caving Club at Penwyllt, with centrally heated changing facilities, showers and a tally board for monitoring all of the expeditions underground in the area.

One Saturday morning, I drove up to Penwyllt to rendezvous with three friends for a trip up the streamway from Ogof Ffynnon Ddu One to Ogof Ffynnon Ddu Two—'One to Two' in the vernacular. Pausing on the bridge over the Newydd at the bottom of the hill to check on the water level, I noticed patches of snow on the banks and on the hillside. It had been the coldest spring for a century and we had received several heavy and unexpected snowfalls in the previous week. Today, however, it was perceptibly warmer and dry weather was forecast. The stream looked surprisingly low, so our proposed route should be safe. In flood, the Nant Newydd is a killer, as several drownings above and below ground testify.

Notional Sketch of OFDI-II traverse

Cross-section of OFD I to II

At Penwyllt I met Tony and Brian who had just arrived from the Potteries after an early start. We chatted, drank tea, munched Brian's biscuits and waited for Dave to arrive to complete our foursome. Dave had last visited Ogof Fynnon Ddu in the late 50's before the main streamway was discovered, so this would be a particularly interesting trip for him. The rest of us had made the traverse many times before, but were looking forward to another enjoyable replay. The rendezvous had been set for 10.00 a.m., so when Dave had still not appeared at 11.30 a.m., we decided to brew another pot of tea, drink it and then change for a noon descent at the latest. We were concerned that he had lost his way, or had an accident en route from Birmingham.

Just as I was pouring out the tea, there was a tap on my shoulder and a jovial voice in my ear. Dave had arrived! He had just bought a new car and had been delayed by the delivery. We were relieved to see him and poured him a cup of tea. After a fag he was ready to change into caving gear and we adjourned to the changing rooms. Dave, resplendent in his recently purchased bright blue wetsuit, pulled on a pair of size 8 black boots borrowed from his school caving club. Compared with the rest of us clad in ancient tatty wetsuits, he looked a veritable whizz-kid! Donning our helmets and lamps, we completed our preparations, left our route details on the marker board and commenced the downhill walk to the lower entrance, about a mile away.

The bottom entrance to Ogof Ffynnon Ddu is tucked away in a cleft behind Y Grithig, a farmstead at the bottom of the hill. By the time that we reached it, we were all warm and our boots more supple from the walk. I climbed the stone wall protecting the entrance, descended the fixed ladders in the hole behind and unlocked the entrance cover. We climbed down into the cave, our eyes slowly adjusting to the darkness.

The first section of the cave had been cleared and pathed for a showcave, so our initial progress was rapid and easy as we passed the various named attractions such as 'The Font' in the 'Cathedral.' Near 'Pluto's bath,' a large green-tinted pool leading to the streamway, we met another party emerging from a short trip around the lower series. We stopped for a chat and then continued on our way, avoiding a wetting by taking an alternative dry route up a slope of gour pools racked vertically like a stone toastrack. At the next junction we turned right into a steeply descending gallery and then, after slithering down past the narrow confines of the 'Loopways' pool, we arrived at 'The Step,' the entry point to the streamway. The 'Step' is the gauge used by cavers to assess whether the water level in the Main Streamway higher up is negotiable. The water was not particularly high on the step, so we plunged into its icy depths and forged upstream against the current. High above us the rift containing the stream reflected the roar of the water in a constant assault on our eardrums. The deep potholes in the streamway were bridged with iron poles to enable us to balance across without falling in. There had been long discussions with the purists about these poles over the years, but after several unilateral attempts to remove them, they had been left in place, ostensibly for beginners or older folk to avoid an unexpected ducking. Passing various side passages and the incoming torrent from the mainstream sump, we soon arrived at the ruckle of boulders in Boulder Chamber.

This was originally the end of the cave, but now there was a way through. We wriggled in between the boulders and chimneyed down to 'Hush' sump, a pool of water in the connection between OFDI and OFD2. The name was apt; it seemed still and quiet, with no sign of the turbulent water flowing underneath. We now had to squirm upwards and forwards through a mass of jumbled rocks until we emerged in a small chamber with a gravelly slope down to 'Dip' Sump. It was through 'Dip' Sump that the cave divers explored the underwater connection to the upper streamway, via a dive of about 200 feet, to discover the enormous system of OFD2 in a succession of epic expeditions which eventually led to the 'Top' entrance being excavated. However, for us, a route bypassing the sump through a low gritty crawl was possible.

This sump bypass had been discovered by digging out rocks and gravel until the bottom of a large pool was broken into that suddenly engulfed the unfortunate diggers in a tidal wave. The large pool behind the blockage finally drained out leaving crystallised shapes in the roof now exposed to view as we emerged to standing height. The crystallised 'stalactites' were quite rare and as Dave had not seen them before, we spent a while inspecting them before proceeding.

The route continued into a shattered region often termed OFD1½ as it was between the two systems. Here we dropped to our stomachs to slide down a small slot and into a dry flat out crawl that eventually emerged into a large passage and a chamber with an obvious climb leading to an upper passageway. Instead of tackling the direct route, we climbed part way up in the chamber to gain a small tortuous crawl that, although safer than a direct climb, made the others complain loudly at its cramped confines. After following the high level passage to a low wet crawl and a series of small dry bedding planes, we dropped out into a large gallery at a T-junction.

Here we detoured to the right to visit Pwll Twll, a large vertical shaft too deep and precipitous to descend without a ladder, but a useful route marker, before returning up the gallery to a complex of passages and climbs leading to a crawl between dangerously loose rocks. Here we had to move very cautiously to pass through to Fault Chamber where we stopped for Dave to recharge with nicotine and have a brief rest before the next section.

Fault Chamber has a sheer wall at an angle of about 60° to the horizontal with a slot at a height of about twenty feet. The gymnastics involved in ascending the steep cliff and inserting one's body into the slot is always a source of amusement to idle observers. The recent addition of a fixed rope certainly helped, however, and we all negotiated the slot safely to reach a jagged rift on the other side that sloped steeply down into a complex of low tubular passages. Following a downward route through the network of crawls, we eventually arrived at a muddy pool across which a hidden connection was located. The squeeze through this was the tightest and most awkward so far, involving a tight left-hand bend into a most annoying and constricted flat out crawl with irregularly shaped holes in the floor, the rock edges of which snagged clothing and tackle, making progress difficult. We squeezed and inched our bodies along on our stomachs for several yards of this constriction to emerge part way down the 'Divers Pitch,' at the head of a vertical descent of about 50 feet.

The 'Divers Pitch' was liberally festooned with jagged hand and footholds making the descent easy if somewhat vertiginous. One by one we climbed to the bottom and continued down a further boulder slope to regroup below. An upwards wriggle behind a large block followed by a climb over more boulders led into a series of enormous galleries where we made rapid progress past several side passages to a vast junction, 'Piccadilly.'

A scramble up to the left led us into the Nether Rawl series of gigantic muddy passages. Here we detoured as far as a flowing cascade to refresh ourselves with the water falling like rain from overhead. Returning to the main Piccadilly junction, we took a slippery climb down into a large passage with flood debris high up its walls. Further on a stream entered from the left at 'The Confluence' and the roof soon lowered to a wide boulder-strewn crawl in the water. Past the crawl we were able to stand up and start wading upstream against the vigorous swirling currents of the Nant Newydd.

The streamway was exhilarating after the monumental gloom and silence of the previous passages. Our voices, raised to overcome the noise of the torrent, echoed between the polished limestone walls. Droplets of water, thrown into the air by our thighs cutting the current, sparkled in the beams of our lamps like fireworks. The streamway twisted and turned as we continued upstream and after a short distance the passageway widened and we climbed up over a rock pile cascading with white water into the First River Chamber, a lofty hall with a rocky beach to catch our breath on. A cigarette later we pushed on once more against the remorseless current. It is said that one never sees the same stream twice as it is forever changing, but the pressure on our legs made us constantly aware of a single presence as we made steady progress upstream.

Then we came to the refreshing slopes of the 'Marble Showers.' A gallery of black limestone inlaid with pure white calcite glistened coldly beautiful in our lights. Wings of water sprouted from our boots as we trod in the stream flowing over the marbled slabs and we each felt the uplift of the music of the water and the aura of light. High above us an inlet disgorged a constant spray of water, adding to the spume around us. Tumbling down from an upper series, the inlet pointed the way to a dry route to the surface, essential knowledge in times of flood. Today we opted for the aqueous delights of the streamway and continued upstream to encounter the first of many deep potholes, this time without poles over them.

The potholes were beautifully round in cross section, milled deep over the centuries by rocks and pebbles held in vortices, the water in some of them green and bottomless. We straddled over these on delicate holds to avoid immersion, occasionally finding the best footholds just below water level. Sometimes we had to jump when no holds could be found. In flood these potholes become extremely dangerous, because of the undertow and because of the difficulty in climbing out against fast running water. At one juncture we rounded a corner after traversing a particularly large pothole and I avoided a smaller hole, but just as deep which followed and stepped on to safe ground. Turning to warn Dave, who was following me, my lamp hid the second hole in bright reflections. He stepped forward, relieved to have passed a major obstacle and with a shout of surprise, disappeared into it! Gasping and spluttering, he surfaced and I grabbed his arm to help him out as he could not swim. Tony and Brian, who had been soaked already, thought this was a great joke and I too found it difficult not to laugh. It's odd how the misfortunes of others seem so amusing! Luckily for me, Dave was quite amiable about it. The potholes soon petered out and we waded into a less exciting streamway, which became brown and sluggish as we approached the Great Oxbow. Here we had to climb out on to dry land to avoid a submerged section of passage. A short quiet passage led to a climb over a rock bridge. The route was then through some static shallow pools and over jammed rocks into a lofty rift passage. Here we were exposed to potential rockfalls that could be displaced by climbers on the dry-route traverse high overhead. Several bends in the passage soon led us back into the torrent again down an awkward straddle over a fifteen-foot climb between slippery walls.

The fine streamway continued, clean and refreshing as ever, with one or two more deep potholes to negotiate and soon beds of dolomite appeared rougher and yellowish grey in comparison with the smooth black limestone. We had barely noticed the steady climb that we were making in the general activity of dealing with the watery obstacles. Now the dolomite beds acted as markers and we could see our progress easily. Progress was particularly rapid as we climbed up a series of small waterfalls caused by the change in rock hardness. We soon reached another inlet running down the left-hand wall from an upper series. This was the Maypole Inlet and the route out of the main streamway to the Top entrance. However, since there was still more of the streamway to see, we continued upstream.

The walls began to close in and the stream ran faster until we reached a low deep pool leading to the boulders preceding the second oxbow where we had to climb out to avoid another sump. On we went up several small cascades and water slides until some time later we neared the Top Waterfall. The Top Waterfall made its presence felt well before we reached it, the ominous roar reverberating along the passages from the water crashing twenty feet into a large pool at its base. The sight and sound of the water was most impressive when we were in the final chamber but it was too cold in the flying spume and cutting wind to linger, so after a final look we returned downstream to the 'Maypole' inlet that we had passed earlier.

The climb out of the streamway was straight up for about fifteen feet via smooth scalloped walls surmounted initially by bridging across the passage, feet on one side, hands on the other, to an ample ledge. The route continued upward on good hand and footholds, to an awkward vertical climb over 'moonmilk' covered rocks running with water. 'Moonmilk' is a white waxy sort of flowstone, extremely soft and greasy and here it presented ample opportunities to slip back down again. The next section was equipped with a fixed steel ladder to surmount a twenty-foot climb into a narrow rift where it was only possible to progress sideways. We wriggled and squeezed along this rift puffing with the exertion to a place where there were jammed rocks and a small inlet on the right.

An upward climb led out of the meandering rift via small slippery ledges to a lefthand bend about ten feet above the floor. The way past this was devoid of hand or footholds and progress was only possible by jamming shoulders and knees on the side walls, aiming to keep at the same level without sliding downwards under gravity. Around the bend was a football-sized chockstone, wedged firmly in the rift which afforded a brief respite before the start of another vertical climb over mud covered boulders jammed in the rift. A convenient ledge about thirty feet up allowed an excellent view of the others below me, but their shouted conversations echoing around the rift were hard to decipher so I continued upwards. The final part of the climb was 'dynamic'—that is, the idea was to move rapidly enough to gain the next hold before slipping off the previous one.

At the top, the climb led into a passage of larger proportions where we regrouped, all of us now liberally smeared in the reddish brown mud typical of the South Wales cave systems. Tony and Brian had muddy warpaint on their faces. Dave's fashionable wetsuit now looked much more workmanlike, the bright colours hidden in a veil of mud. The way led to a short crawl on the right along a muddy tube to a deep hole in the floor which we crossed on a muddy ledge to a small round chamber with fluted walls of flowstone reaching high above us into the gloom. At first sight it looked like a dead end, but a hidden exit led to the 'Crossroads' where we stopped to decide on the best way to the surface and allow Dave another fag.

We were now in the upper series of Ogof Ffynnon Ddu II and could choose several exit routes through the complex of passages. To our right was 'Salubrious' passage, the shortest route to the surface with a small stream in it. To our left a boulderstrewn descent led over deep holes in the floor to the dry and sandy 'Selenite' passage named after its Selenite formations. Dave wanted to see the formations so we turned left, traversed the holes and were soon admiring the sparkling walls and ceilings of 'Selenite' passage. Some of the formations had yellow tints, some were orange-red and some were surrounded by white crystalline masses like icing sugar. With its sandy floor the passage had a calm serenity of its own and we strolled through it in a pleasant silence after the roar of the stream, taking great care not to touch the formations.

Turning to the right past a shattered pillar supporting the roof, we straddled over another hole in the floor, and then puffed and panted up a steep passage with a sandy floor that eventually lowered to a crawl and a 'Tee' junction in a large corridor. Left led us past the 'Red Crystal Pool,' its beauty long gone under the dust of countless visitors, and then over yet another hole and up a steep slope of huge boulders to a short crawl and another 'Tee' junction. Here we again turned left to a further junction where fresh water was dripping from the ceiling in a large chamber on the left.

Any reader not yet bored by the detail will have gathered that the Upper Series of Ogof Ffynnon Ddu Two is quite complex and littered with deep holes in the floor. In fact this is the case, because after slaking our thirst in the chamber we turned and took the passage ahead past some red and muddy formations to a slippery traverse over yet another deep hole in the floor. Here there had recently been a serious accident when a caver had slipped and nearly killed himself, ricochetting down between the walls to the bottom, so we took particular care at this point. We climbed over the hole and into a small chamber with two ways on and took a narrow ledge left into 'Edward's Shortcut.'

This was a medium-sized passage with progress over, around and under boulders, with a slippery climb upwards at one point before a final crawl into the blackness of 'Gnome' passage.

Progress along 'Gnome' passage was relatively easy and we climbed over the large boulders littering the floor of a cavern that was at least fifty feet high and twenty to thirty feet wide. As we made our way up this huge gallery, our lights reflected off small stumpy stalagmites peering at us from amongst the rocks like garden gnomes. We surmised that this was the reason for the appellation 'Gnome Passage.'

At the end of Gnome Passage the route became more complex with several junctions and well-worn boulder-strewn routes to follow until we emerged near 'Big Chamber Near the Entrance,' a large chamber on our right so unimaginatively but aptly named. We could smell the entrance now and, passing a group of stalagmite pillars, we were soon on the steep gravelly slope that ended at the small ovenlike door guarding the Top Entrance.

To our surprise the door opened under a large snowdrift and we had to crawl through a snowtube to the surface. How glad we were that we did not have to dig the snow out ourselves! I wondered how the door had been opened under the weight of snow in the first place. Dave and Brian crawled out into the daylight and we stood looking at the superb view of the Welsh valley below until Tony joined us, clanging the door shut behind him. All aglow and pleased with our sporting traverse, we walked downhill to the warm showers in the club hut.

Like countless cavers before us, we had let the Nant Newydd wash the everyday world from our minds for a while and were now released, refreshed and ready for an evening's entertainment.

14

Helictite Heaven

The 1981 International Caving Conference in Kentucky was a positive stimulus for many cavers to go caving in America during the summer. However, business commitments prevented me from attending, so I decided to visit Alabama in October instead. This was a fortunate decision as the weather is more clement in the fall, prices are lower and Alabama has more subterranean variety than Kentucky. Eventually, after a great deal of planning and thanks to the Huntsville Grotto and Sir Freddie Laker, I was able to afford a week's caving with my family in between visiting the French Quarter in New Orleans and a fortnight's tour of sunny Florida.

We stayed in Alabama as houseguests of Bill and Louise Varnedoe, veteran members of the Huntsville Grotto. Their large modern house on Green Mountain, high above Huntsville, was situated in thick woodland with a superb view over the Tennessee Valley. Bill and Louise not only provided food and accommodation for Dilys, Catherine and myself, but also organised caving and touring trips and even a grotto party. We had heard of Southern hospitality before but were overwhelmed by their kindness.

The limestone in the Huntsville area has sandstone capping and almost horizontal bedding. Over two thousand cave systems have been recorded and Bill gave me details of the computerised data bank that he had set up to handle the records. The surface featured several flat-topped hills rising to about 1500 ft. above the valley of the Tennessee River and merging northwards into the Cumberland Plateau. These hills, called mountains locally, were all clad in deciduous forest, the October colours providing an unforgettable spectacle of brilliant reds and fiery orange. The undergrowth was dense in places and well supplied with sawbriers, poison ivy and other clutching and clawing shrubbery. Mountain lions, racoons, skunks, rattlers, deer and even bears are reputed to inhabit the woods but are rarely seen due to their shyness of humans.

In the caves we were also amazed at the variety of subterranean denizens. We saw hundreds of cave crickets, several salamanders, crayfish, bats and once a large pack rat. Shelta cave that runs under the National Speleological Society library in the centre of Huntsville had an abundance of blind fish in its waters.

Our first caving trip was to Tumbling Rock Cave about forty miles from Huntsville, near Scottsboro. We made an early start, stopping to buy some wellies for Catherine and to pick up Chuck Lundquist, another veteran caver, and arrived at the cave before the heat of the day had time to develop. After signing an indemnity chit and paying a small fee at the landowner's cabin, we changed at the roadside and entered the cave nearby.

Inside the cave entrance it was immediately noticeable that the atmosphere was considerably warmer than in British caves. Very soon I began to overheat in my Damarts and waterproof overalls. About a thousand feet in, we paused to examine an old Saltpetre working, a relic of the American Civil War. Here, I stripped off my thick underwear and left it on a convenient ledge nearby for collection on the way out. The passageway continued wide and high, with an uncluttered floor, and we made rapid progress, passing some large columns shaped like elephant's feet, until the way was blocked by a large boulder ruckle. A period of crawling and wriggling followed until we emerged into a tunnel leading to 'Totem Gallery' with its beautiful columns reminiscent of Indian totem poles.

I took some photographs and we climbed down into a roomy bedding plane followed by a complex of small tubular passages and one or two damp sections. At the original 'Tumbling rock' boulder choke, we again had to crawl and negotiate several climbs, although under more stable conditions than those experienced by the early explorers. Eventually we were able to stand upright again and soon entered a huge cavern named 'Allen's Alley,' its floor a jumble of rocks and massive boulders. Towards the end of this passage, up on the right-hand wall, was a most rare and unexpected cave phenomenon, a tar spring called the 'Asphalt Ooze.' The shiny treaclelike substance dripped lugubriously from the roof onto the boulders below, its glistening mass a trap for unfortunate cave crickets.

Catherine felt hungry, so she and Chuck sat down to lunch on sausages, fruit and sweets, whilst Bill and I continued further on to scale the muddy and precipitous slopes of 'Mount Olympus.' We free climbed several exposed slabs and about a hundred feet above the floor of 'Allen's Alley' we came to the 'Pillar of Fire,' an enormous stalactite with a fat, pointed, dome striped with bright red pigmentation. Balancing on the slippery, almost vertical slope alongside, I took some photos of Bill on the flat shelf with the formation, and then we climbed carefully down to rejoin the others. I took several photos of the asphalt and we started the return journey.

In the complex at the end of 'Allen's Alley' we detoured and mantleshelfed up through a hole in the roof to gain a passage encrusted with 'popcorn' formations where there were some rare black calcite flows with white 'spilt milk' on the surface. Rejoining the main route again we continued out, pausing only to take photographs and to allow Catherine the occasional rest *(She was only ten years old after all!)*. We emerged into the coolness of the evening, pleasantly tired and surprisingly clean.

The next day, I went out with John French also of the Huntsville grotto, to drop into some pits on Montesano Mountain. We drove into the woods along a rough track and warmed up with a descent of 'Hooper's Well'—a ninety-foot drop alongside a thirty-foot stalactite. Before the descent John scanned the ledges near the surface for rattlers, probably for my benefit rather than in expectation of seeing one. Suitably warm, we then decamped to another area on Montesano and after a downhill scramble located 'Natural Well'—a superb open shaft with smooth limestone walls descending 180 ft. to a rubble cone and a thousand feet of passage. The aptly named 'Cathedral' below the rubble cone was a huge rift, its beautiful white walls soaring upwards into the blackness. In the traverses and crawls below, the dust was considerable and thoughts of contracting a dose of *Histoplasmosis* crossed my mind, so I was glad to return to the daylight. The freehanging ascent was pleasurable except for the last twenty feet where the sweat ran into my eyes. American pits are really hot!

The most interesting day's outing involved a voyage up Flint Creek, near Hartselle, in Chuck's canoe. It was a cloudy day with showers so the two or three miles of paddling clad in our caving gear were not marred by mosquitoes or heavy perspiration. Bill wielded the front paddle and kept an eye out for submerged logs and rocks. Dilys and Catherine sat amidships, I sat behind with the second paddle and Chuck perched in the stern steered with the third paddle, using his weight to trim the canoe. After a journey reminiscent of those made by the early settlers, we beached the canoe near the bluffs containing Anvil Cave.

We just had time to drag the canoe into the undergrowth and invert it before a heavy downpour drove us scuttling for cover in the cave mouth. A low crawl led us into an incredible maze of passages. Bill gave us a set of 'rally' instructions typed in four languages that had been used for a Congress competition. Visitors had to negotiate a series of checkpoints in a target time. Since there were several entrances to the system, the most amusing clues were those out in the open which led the confused victims from one entrance to another. Catherine led the way and we scrambled after her, following the route past several easily recognised landmarks including a set of bear claw scrapes, to somewhere in the middle of the maze. Here we lunched on Chuck's tinned sausages again before trying to find the way out. At several junctions we each took different routes but eventually all of us regained the entrance by which we had entered.

We launched the canoe, reembarked and paddled downstream. En route we stopped several times to investigate small streams and bluffs on the left-hand bank of the creek, prospecting for new caves. I actually discovered a small one, to the intense delight of Catherine, who was used to inspect a small tube from which a draught issued. Bill and Chuck made a rapid survey of its vast extent for the records and we then had to abandon further promising areas and return to Huntsville as time was pressing for an evening engagement.

For myself, the highlight of the holiday was a descent of Fern Cave. I had hoped to abseil down 'Surprise Pit'—a drop of over four hundred feet—but a 'superior' trip had been planned via another entrance to avoid humping rope up the jungly hillside in the heat. Over a hearty breakfast of bacon, eggs, 'grits,' pancakes and coffee in Gibson's Cafe in Huntsville, I met the cavers: 'J.V.', the leader, and his father 'Van' together with Avis, John and two of their visitors, Russ from New Jersey and Pakwan from Thailand. After the usual delays, 'J.V.' eventually managed to load up his huge truck and we drove out along the route to Scottsboro.

Turning off the state highway, we crossed a creek by a very rickety old bridge and then took a rough track to park below a steep wooded hillside. We changed quickly and 'J.V.' pushed off into the undergrowth, the rest of us struggling behind him. Very soon he was out of sight and we were lost. We shouted "Boh!" *(Signifying I'm here. Where are you?)*. A faint "Boh, Boh!" *(I'm over here)* came from high above to our left. We circled and climbed, tugging at vines, sawbriers and shrubs that hampered our movements. 'J.V.' was far too fit for comfort! Finally we broke out onto an old logging trail which contoured around the mountain. In response to a volley of "Bohs" we obtained "Boh, BOH, BOH!" *(Come here quickly)* and following the sound, soon located 'J.V.' sitting on a log near the Fern Sink. The entrance was under a small cliff, peatblackened, dripping with moisture, and steaming in the sunshine.

Fiddling with the carbide lamps belonging to Russ and Avis took some time and a wild grapevine heavy with *'auslese'* black grapes delayed us, but eventually we scrambled down into the sink and followed a small streamway to the head of 'Surprise Pit.' The deep hole had an aura of depth about it and we respectfully traversed around the lip to gain a large platform for a better view. We dropped a few stones into the void and listened to the distant echoes from far below. Our curiosity satisfied, we returned to the surface. It would have been an exhilarating abseil, but we were off to 'Helictite Heaven' for visual rather than adrenal stimulation.

A short walk along the same contour and we came to 'Johnson's Entrance,' a small slot in the wall of a large ravine. 'J.V.' and I entered first with the tackle and we climbed down through a boulder choke into a series of large bedding caves well decorated with muddy speleothems. We made one or two detours to inspect pits in the floor and to locate the connection to the Northern Series before entering a phreatic passage with a vadose trench hiding the imperceptible 'Bolt Drop.' 'J.V.' belayed an ancient piece of 'Bluewater' rope to a large rock flake and we abseiled down through a small hole into a circular pit about forty feet deep. At the bottom we removed our gear as the rest of the trip was free climbable and waited for the others.

They were slow arriving so I explored down the next pitch into a rift chamber, taking an easy route to the left ending at another deep pit. Eventually the others arrived and we climbed down a more difficult route to the right into a deep rift. With 'J.' leading, we traversed along this rift for a considerable distance. The rift was about two hundred feet deep, but had plenty of footholds. In some sections there were beautiful encrustations of gypsum crystal, in others heaps of loose rubble and fragile rock flakes. After some time we took a downward chimney to gain access to a lower series of small crumbly tunnels full of loose rock. A tightish vertical slot dropped us into a large chamber, glittering with Gypsum crystals. The largest crystal that I have ever seen protruded from the roof. It was more than four feet long like a sculpted Christmas tree. I was distracted from looking closer at it, however, by a minor crisis in the slot. John had become tightly wedged and was calling for assistance.

Whilst the others tried to extrude John through the slot, I took the opportunity to take some photographs. I had plenty of time as John was heavily built and took some shifting. Luckily he seemed to be compressible and after removing most of his clothes, was forced through in one piece. He pulled himself together and we took a low, dry and very shattered passage that ended in a crawl into the bedding planes of the fabulous 'Helictite Heaven.'

Bushes of curved helictites sprouted from the floor, dazzling white crystal stars glittered from the walls and as far as one could see helictites writhed and twisted in a profusion that was unbelievable. This was not all. A letterbox allowed access to a deep rift thatched with helictites and crystals. A short traverse then led to a succession of beautifully embroidered chambers and spectacular grottoes all pristine white and prickly with crystals and curving speleothems. I tried to decide what to photograph, at the same time trying to etch an indelible impression on my memory.

By the time that I had used up all my film, the others were ready to leave. After gathering up the photographic gear, we crawled back into the drab connecting passage still dazzled by what we had seen. The journey back to the surface was uneventful although lengthy. John negotiated the tight slot with no trouble. 'J.V.' eventually found the return route on to the traverses and after ascending the 'Bolt Drop' we passed the entrance series to emerge into pitch darkness. The scramble down through the woods in the dark was memorable, the snags and pitfalls worse than any underground, but we finally made it back to the truck, scratched and torn to change out of our caving clothes. A convivial evening followed to complete a superb day's caving.

Apart from the caving trips, we packed in several excellent walks, a tour of the Huntsville Space Centre and a visit to Nashville, so our holiday passed incredibly quickly. Suddenly it was time to leave. We were sorry to say goodbye to Bill and Louise and hoped our farewells would be *'au revoir'* and not *'Adieu'*. As we drove away southwards through the cottonfields we looked back at the wooded Alabama Hills and knew that we would never forget our holiday there.

15

The Hall of the Thirteen

Sketched from a photograph by Trevor Faulkner

The campfire crackled and spat. Sparks whirled high on a shimmering plume of hot air and wood smoke. In the circle of firelight at the boundary between comfortable warmth and scorching heat sat forty cavers in various states of sobriety. Our expedition had 'bottomed' the Gouffre Berger, one of the world's deepest caves and the celebrations were well in hand. After several days of strenuous effort ferrying rope and provisions over the mountain and down the cave to feed the riggers we could now take a well-earned rest. However, with all the pitches rigged to the bottom, there was enough time left for a few 'fun' trips before the harder task of detackling started.

Lenny, Brian and I discussed such a trip. How pleasant it would be to float down the cave with the bare essentials of light and food, unencumbered by heavy sacks of rope and ironmongery! Unanimously we decided that tomorrow was the chance, we would have a fun trip down the Berger. Without more ado we abandoned the revelry and crept off to our tents in order to be ready for an early start in the morning.

We all slept well that night, in spite of the prospect of the Berger in our minds. Certain words can evoke particular images of their own. The word 'Berger,' to most cavers, conjures up visions of the vast cavern of 'The Hall of The Thirteen' with its stalagmites rising out of the darkness like eternal monuments to the passage of time. Allied with the beauty there is also the thought of the arduous passages and deep pitches that have to be overcome.

Cavers have different expectations from the Berger. Some visit the cave out of curiosity, some seeking fun, some to capture its beauty on film and some to prove themselves in a macho world of their own. My aim was to realise a youthful dream…I wanted to recapture the emotions and sensations of the early explorers that I had read about years before. For me the bottom of the cave was a group objective and not a personal one. What was an initiation rite for some was for me the maturation of an idea. Mellowed by wine and warmth, I soon fell asleep.

The morning mist was still thick and cold when we roused ourselves. A hearty communal breakfast soon dispelled the morning chill, however, and soon we were kitted up and walking briskly over the plateau to the Gouffre Berger. The familiar route through the forest was soon completed and we arrived at the entrance just as the sun started to break through. We checked our caving gear, buckled on our harnesses, lit our lamps and descended the entrance pitch. The snow at the bottom was as icy as ever so I moved on to the shaky wooden platform over the Ruiz shaft, clipped my rack into the rope and slid rapidly thirty metres to the bottom. Then on down the 'Holiday' slides to Cairn pitch into Cairn Hall, all of us now part of a flying rhythm of descent, our light tackle bags a permit for enjoyment.

The 'Meanders' were a doddle unencumbered and we whizzed down Garby's and Gontard's shafts, down the 'Relay' pitches to the top of Aldo's fifty-metre shaft. As I traversed out over the long drop, Brian and Lenny arrived behind me. There were two ropes on Aldo's: Brian used the nearest, I the furthest, but I hit the bottom first and forty minutes from the entrance we reached the dried out Lake Cadoux. Just half an hour later, having passed the Bourgin Hall, Little General, the Tyrolienne and the Great Rubble Heap, we arrived breathless at the Mecca of cavers, the Hall of the Thirteen. Our exhilarating descent was ample compensation for the sweaty grind of previous Sherpa trips. This certainly was a fun trip!

Rising from the musty dump of Camp One, Kevin, Tony, Liam and Phil, who had spent the night there, were surprised to see us. Lenny commandeered a primus stove and soon we were fishing meatballs, dehydrated vegetables, potato mush and gobbets of unidentifiable fat and gristle from the bubbling gravy in a large mess tin. Fortified by the meal, we decided to join Liam and Phil who were on their way to the bottom. Brian borrowed a wetsuit and 'just in case' we booked two sleeping bags on the proviso that we would take them out later. Lenny had to be out of the cave in time to catch a ferry so dispensed with both on the grounds that he would have no time to use either!

Five in number, we crossed the Hall of Thirteen and were soon at the Balcony pitch. A cautious descent and one by one we slithered down the 'Vestibule' pitch which followed, to regroup at the start of the watery 'Couffinades.' A momentary pause to adjust our lamps and organise our wetsuits and we were on the move again, Lenny traversing to keep out of the icy water, the rest of us splashing through with gay abandon. We were now in the active streamway with rushing water and noisy cascades, the atmosphere of the sparkling torrent refreshing and exciting. Soon we had straddled the iron pole over Claudine's Cascade and were shooting down to the deep pool below.

More waterways to the Topographers cascade and then we were into the dryness of the steeply sloping Grand Canyon, with the water running deep in a ravine on the left. We had been travelling fast and light again, but it was a difficult descent and some time elapsed before we slithered to a halt at the bottom. Here at Camp Two a food and first aid dump had been established so we sat down to decide what to do next. There were only three more big pitches to the bottom, so Lenny decided to carry on down with Phil and Liam. Brian and I, however, decided that we would make a leisurely return to Camp One, taking a closer look at the passageways that we had rushed through during our descent. In any case, if Lenny wanted to get out quickly enough to catch his ferry, we would have to help with his tackle and could prepare a meal for him to save time. We wished the others 'Bon Voyage' as they disappeared into the darkness and commenced the steep climb out. It was most pleasant to be able to take our time to inspect grottoes, watch the waterfalls and examine the noisy 'elephant's doodah' at close quarters and the ascent passed most enjoyably.

By the time that we reached the Hall of Thirteen, both of us were beginning to feel the effects of a long and eventful day. It was approaching nine p.m. as we passed the group of silent stalagmites looming out of the darkness like giant sentinels, and when we reached Camp One it was deserted. We took off our wetsuits and dried ourselves on paper towels before putting on our 'furry' suits, still slightly damp from our descent of the morning. We had at least four hours to kill before Lenny's arrival, so we decided to eat a meal and to try and catch some sleep. Our 'fun' trip had consumed more time and energy than we had planned and I for one relished the prospect of a comfy sleeping bag. Brian lit a primus stove and I went to fetch water from the gour pools in the Hall of the Thirteen.

Under the stony gaze of the calcite guardians, I scooped water from the clearest gour pool, my senses alert like an animal at a waterhole. A deep impenetrable silence surrounded me and the chill air seemed to enclose me in a still and timeless hold. Camp One seemed far away and in contrast to the headlong speed and excitement of the morning, the tranquillity of the vast hall calmed my thoughts. I was aware of crossing a bridge between past and future. For many years I had dreamt of visiting this place and now I was here, the reality meeting my expectations. Soon I would depart, a transient being in this remote and lifeless sanctuary from the outside world, carrying memories into the future. Caught in the spell of the numinous, motionless and poised in thought, I allowed myself to absorb the scene for as long as I was able, then carefully holding the mess tin to avoid spilling its precious contents I returned to Camp One.

Brian was in his sleeping bag already, warming another meaty concoction on the stove from a reclining position on one elbow. Our meal was soon prepared, eaten and washed down with hot chocolate brewed from the water that I had collected. After placing my wetsuit to cushion me from the rocky floor I slid into my borrowed bag, damp and clammy as it was, to keep warm. A pleasant tingling sensation invaded my feet as I relaxed horizontally and prepared for sleep. The flame on my lamp was only a guttering glimmer now and as I closed my eyes I felt a wave of tiredness run through me. Within seconds I was asleep—in the Hall of the Thirteen.

16

"Allumez le feu"

Region of wooded hills, sparkling rivers, lush meadows and limestone gorges, the Jura FrancheComte is a caver's paradise. The magnificent Reseau du Verneau, the aqueous Chauveroche, the mysterious Pourpevelle and the thousand spiky columns of the Grange Mathieu are but a few of the subterranean delights on hand to whet the caver's appetite.

To complement the pleasure of a day's caving, the local cuisine tempts the palate with recipes for freshwater fish, game and dairy produce that match the refreshing light wines of the region—an opportunity for speleology in Arcadia!

The Jura FrancheComte was the setting for one of the most idyllic summer outings that I can remember. It started midmorning when the sun had started to dispel the early scented air. Several of us, who were holidaying in the area, rendezvoused at the hamlet of Chenecy Buillon. We planned to descend the beautiful cave of Grange Mathieu nearby. We parked our cars under the trees to shade them from the sun and then gathered at the chalet of Monsieur Ehinger, nicknamed *'Le Trappeur.'* *'Le Trappeur'* was the discoverer and owner of the cave and would be our guide.

Our group consisted of six families in all, fielding a dozen wouldbe cavers and five determined noncavers. After some discussion with *'Le Trappeur'* and payment of a small fee, we changed into old clothes, boots and caving helmets. *'Le Trappeur'* was emphatic that we would not need our acetylene cap-lamps, but several of us took them as a matter of habit. Two of us took photographic equipment as well, hoping to capture some of the expected beauty on film.

We assembled at the head of the treelined entrance pitch. This was a large crater about ten metres in diameter and about twenty-five metres deep, with a rubble cone below, clearly visible in the sunlight streaming down through the trees. *'Le Trappeur'* rigged up a *Treuil,* or winch, fitted with a simple sling for a seat, whilst Keith, Derek and I belayed a rope to a tree for abseiling. An electron ladder was also attached to a tree and dropped down the shaft, giving a triple diversity descent for our motley crew of cavers.

One by one we descended the entrance pitch. Roselyn, Claude, Cecile and Frederick were lowered on the winch. Keith, Derek, Yannick, Catherine, Frédérique, Mike and I abseiled down the rope. *'Le Trappeur'* remained at the surface, directing operations until we were all down.

This was Mike's first caving trip and he found the start memorable, as he had never abseiled before. I could share some of his feelings as he jerked awkwardly down the rope, trying to control his rate of fall in perilous and unfamiliar circumstances. The descents took some time, so we were glad when *'Le Trappeur'* finally arrived after swinging hand over hand down the ladder to join us. He produced a set of keys to open the grille over the entrance to the passages below and unlocked the gate to his cave. After the original explorations had been completed, he had purchased the cave and installed some rudimentary electric lighting and fixed aids for caving groups such as ours. For our small fee we were assured of an 'official' visit, arranged by Yannick on our behalf. 'Cave pirates' would have to squeeze past the exit grille for their nocturnal freebies.

Somewhere inside the darkness of the cave, *'Le Trappeur'* threw a switch to turn on the lights. We followed him down a slippery slope, through a narrow passage and then down some iron steps driven into the rock. In a long file behind him, we slid down a short rubble slope and then walked along a large dry passage to point where a fixed steel ladder led up into the roof. Each adult climbed shielding a child directly above, as a psychological rather than an objective safety precaution. The step off the ladder at the top, with a fifteen-metre drop below, was quite hazardous, but we all crossed this without incident.

Keith and I were already beginning to spot some photogenic pictures. The two of us stopped to photograph the fine decorations, ignoring the remarks of *'Le Trappeur'* that we were wasting our film. He told us that there were better sights to come. Our photography took longer than usual because of the electric lights. These were scattered at long irregular intervals and presented quite a problem of film exposure. We were used to photography in pitch darkness, where we could leave the shutters of our cameras open until the flash bulbs lit. Here we had to synchronise shutter and flash.

'Le Trappeur' shouted to us from the distance, his voice echoing and booming down the cave. He was determined to hurry us along. We took our pictures and hastened to join the main party, moving quickly along a semicircular passage, passing stalactites, stalagmites and flowstone bosses that lit up in a white profusion. We were dazzled by the incredible array of calcite. It was a fairy-tale scene, with so much beauty on all sides that it was too much to contemplate. The passage narrowed, and we took some more photographs before hurrying to catch up with the others. They were carefully negotiating a series of small flowstone-covered climbs fitted with wire hand-lines.

Mike and the girls were all enjoying themselves in this wonderland, oblivious to the significant drops below as *'Le Trappeur,'* Yannick and Derek carefully ushered them along. As we advanced, so the formations became more prolific and beautiful and our eyes were dazzled with a surfeit of beauty. Starbursts sparkled on the ceiling. Icing embellished the walls. Needles, columns, curtains and pendulous breasts of flowstone reared on all sides. We stopped to gaze up at an extremely tall and spindly column stretching high up to the roof. White and crystalline from top to bottom it sparkled in the blackness, like a fantastically elongated minaret. However, a greater surprise was in store for us!

A brief walk through a less well-decorated section led us into 'The Hall of a Thousand Columns.' The magical scenery here reduced us to silence. Our perceptive powers almost blown, we walked with mouths agape between graceful white columns on all sides. There were literally a thousand columns there, close packed, tall and shapely, rising from two to ten metres in height. Our flashbulbs exploded their shadows apart in brief bursts of light that bounced from column to column and wall to wall in blinding glory. It was time to sit down and allow our retinas to imbed this beauty in our brain cells.

We had been underground for about three hours now and in French caving protocol, some refreshment was now required. As we opened our bags and unwrapped our snacks, the conversations started again. Mike inquired if all caves were like this. I hesitated to tell him that this extravaganza was exceptional. This, his first trip, could be positively misleading and the mud and gloom in many English caves a letdown. Whilst the others ate and drank, Keith and I engaged in a feast of photography. It was difficult to choose the best shots and we arranged several complicated lighting schemes. Both of us were extremely busy in amongst that splendid scenery that we almost ignored whilst solving our technical problems.

It was not long before our flash bulbs were exhausted and our rations consumed. We reluctantly agreed that it was time to journey back to the entrance. Keith and I realised that 'Le Trappeur' had been right: we should have photographed on the way out and not on the way in. As we returned, stopping from time to time to refresh our memories of some particular beauty, our group spread out leaving 'Le Trappeur' and me at the rear. Our conversation developed as we exchanged caving anecdotes and experiences of particular systems that we had explored. In this manner, we became so absorbed that we barely noticed the beauty of the cave diminishing as we went. At one point, 'Le Trappeur' suddenly decided that if we were to eat on our return to the surface, then the barbecue fires should be kindled as soon as possible.

He walked over to the nearest electric light, removed the bulb and screwed in a connector to a telephone set that he was carrying in his tackle bag. By modulating the electric current, he contacted the non-cavers on the surface. It was either Jenny or Sue who answered the call. *"Allumez le feu"* said *'Le Trappeur.'* "What?" said Jenny. *"Allumez le feu!"* Silence. *'Le Trappeur'* turned the handle. Still silence. *"Allumez le feu!"* he shouted. No response. *'Le Trappeur'* unplugged the phone, muttering in some local dialect. I hoped that Sue had overheard the call as she had fluent French, and I had a developing appetite! *'Le Trappeur'* and I continued to the surface, once more deep in conversation.

Our return to the base of the entrance pitch was uneventful. We emerged into the gaudy sunlight streaming down the shaft. We wasted no time and started to organise the ascent. Keith, Derek and I used our ascenders to climb up our single rope and arrive at the top first. We were then able to help raise the rest of our party, whilst Yannick stayed below to help them into their safety gear. Mike insisted on climbing the ladder, life-lined from above. This proved more troublesome than he had imagined, as a flexible ladder is much harder to climb than a rigid one! Catherine and Fred climbed out after him with practiced ease, whilst the others were winched up in idle luxury. After locking the grille and ascending the ladder, *'Le Trappeur'* went with Yannick to inspect the barbecues that were fortunately alight. Keith, Derek and I de-rigged the pitch and returned to the cars to change into clean clothes. Claude, Roselyn, Pat, Jenny, and Sue started to prepare the food, helped by Judith and Elizabeth.

Trestle tables and benches were erected under the trees near the barbecue pits and Yannick drove his 'camping car' up alongside. The 'camping car' was a veritable treasure chest, containing food, wine, caving implements, ironmongery and all sorts of useful *bricabrac* like bottle openers, bits of wire, *brochettes* and tin foil. Once the cavers returned, clean and tidy again, everyone set to work: cutting *baguettes,* washing salads, pricking sausages, opening wine bottles, turning various meats on the fire and so on. The hustle and bustle increased as the wine was sampled. Claude had some homemade *Cassis* and, with white wine, produced *'Kir'* as an aperitif.

Eventually, the womenfolk had the tables laid and called us all to order from impromptu attacks on the buffet. Yannick unearthed some excellent red Beaune wine from the depths of his van, which we supplemented with local Arbois and Jura wines. *Côtelets de porc, Merguez, Saucisse, Saucisson,* cheese and heaps of fresh salad and bread were passed around to provide a feast spiced by our hunger and the open air. A most convivial meal continued well into the afternoon. The level of conversation rose, our cheeks ruddy from the effects of the wine and occasional visits to tend the barbecue.

After some considerable time, the barbecue began to empty and the eating stopped. Replete and drowsy, we leant back in our chairs. A pleasant stillness enveloped us. We had been drawn together by the magic of the cave and transformed into a closely-knit group by its enchantment. Now we were emerging from a communal meal to sense the day around us. Our nostrils savoured the breath of summer and our limbs relaxed in a warm lassitude. We were caught in a drowsy mood of well-being. It seemed timeless to me and I could easily have gone to sleep. However, Claude, with a flicker of energy, aroused us all. She suggested a short stroll to a local *point de vue* to aid our digestion.

Leaving the tables, we ambled companionably through the hazel thickets and out among the beeswept grasses,. patterned with flowers and butterflies. The hazy path led out to a promontory overlooking the River Loue where we settled down in the grass to admire the view. Far below, the river flowed lazily in a long deep bend, cut slowly through the centuries. Ripples and eddies in the river glinted in the sunlight. The sights seemed mellowed and diffuse, like the soft forms in a romantic film. We were in a Corot painting, close together and linked by invisible brush strokes into a complete ensemble, one relaxed and easy mood of a shared experience. Time passed slowly as we lay in the grass, so slowly…that the moment lasts forever…

17

Three thousand feet up, three thousand feet down

Engine roaring, our tiny monoplane fought its way up the Biggin Hill runway, wartime launch pad of 'The Few.' Although our caving gear and spare clothes were cut to the minimum, the weight of ourselves, our inflight sandwiches and the fuel in the wing-tanks took the allup weight to the limit and our takeoff run was three times the normal. Eventually we were airborne and Ron Crocker, our pilot, set course for the Channel over the Seaford beacon. Our flight to the Pyrenees had begun.

During the next fifty-two hours, I often had to pinch myself to see if the scenes and events were real, as almost everything seemed unbelievable. The idea of traversing the Pierre St. Martin over a weekend, using a light plane to fly there and back, had been dreamt up a year ago, one wine and woodsmoke scented evening on the Sornin Plateau. Around the campfire, Bill Brooks, Andy Ive and I were celebrating a trip down the Gouffre Berger and as the wine flowed, so did our future plans. I said I could arrange to have the P.S.M. booked and rigged and Bill reckoned he could organise a plane, so it seemed feasible. As 1984 unrolled, our plans matured and were finalised. I telephoned my old caving friend Michel in the Pyrenees and Bill spoke to Ron, an expupil of his who owned a four-seater Rallye Tobago 10. Both Michel and Ron were keen to help and the descent was fixed for the first of September. Now, after all the planning, here we were airborne into adventure!

At first the plane seemed very insubstantial. Flying at three thousand feet, we dropped into the occasional airpocket leaving our stomachs momentarily poised mid-air; also, from time to time, the plane seemed to slip sideways. It was completely different from the familiar and stable platform of a scheduled airliner. As the drone of the engine and the voices on the intercom became more usual, we began to notice the lack of legroom and the heat of the sun through the canopy. I idly perused the instrument panel, trying to decipher the digits on the navigation computer, in between watching the landscape below and shouting to Andy, sitting next to me in the back seat.

By the time we crossed into France, high over Le Havre, I was well accustomed to the scene and the motion and started to show interest in our route, using maps provided by Bill. We flew for about three hours, mainly following electric pylons, roads and rivers, with occasional towns like Le Mans acting as waymarkers, until we touched down at Poitiers to clear customs and top up the fuel tanks. A brief chat with the local gendarmes who were standing in for the *douanier* and we were off again, anxious to make our final landing before dusk. We only just made it. The shadows on the ground were lengthening and the sun very low on the horizon when we reached the Pyrenees. We eventually made out the grass landing strip at OloronHerrere, with its corrugated control tower roof carrying the faded letters 'OLORON—HERRERE' picked out in white on the rusty surface.

The control tower appeared to be unmanned. No one answered the radio, so Ron circled for a closer look, especially as there was a powered glider attempting to take off. We buckled on our seat belts and Ron brought us in over the treetops to a neat but bumpy landing on the sunbaked surface. We could see Michel and his wife Annie with their small daughter Laurette over by the car park waving to us. Ron taxied over, and as soon as the engine stopped we clambered out to greet them. For me it was a most pleasant reunion as I had not seen Michel and Annie for four years in which time Laurette had been born, Michel had shaved his beard and I had grown one! We had lots to talk about. However, dinner was waiting back at Michel's new house, so we unloaded our gear from the plane and into the boots of the two cars nearby. We then climbed aboard and Michel and Annie drove us to their home at Issor, leaving the plane parked like a car on the edge of the grassy runway.

Michel's new house was magnificent. High on the side of the valley over Issor, it commanded a superb panoramic view of the Pyrenees. In the twilight we could see the peaks silhouetted against the sky and the mountain air seemed cool and fruity. We walked along a terrace and into the main living room through sliding glass doors, to find Michel's brother JeanPaul and his wife Jaqui putting the final touches to a wellladen dinner table. Gilbert and JeanGilles, old friends from previous caving trips, were cooking sausages on a barbecue near their tent in the garden and, hearing our voices, came in to welcome us. Annie offered Pernod and we all partook of welliced aperitifs, the babble of the conversation increasing as news was exchanged and introductions made. Adding to the throng were JeanPaul's children and Michel's older daughter Anna, who arrived with Michel's enormous sheepdog from a game in the garden.

Annie eventually had us seated around the table and served cold meats and a superb salad laced with raw chilis. "*Un peu épice*" she said as we gasped. Luckily the *mergeuz* sausages were not as hot as usual or we would have sunk even more wine to cool our mouths. Bill gobbled up the chilis as if they were lettuces...he must have had an iron mouth! We had a most enjoyable dinner during which Michel explained the details of what had been arranged for the traverse. Two days previously Michel, JeanPaul, Gilbert and JeanGilles had rigged all the pitches from the entrance via Tête Sauvage to the bottom. They had arranged transport, too. Gilbert's car was already at St. Engrâce, at the end of the traverse. We would travel to Tête Sauvage in Michel's old car and in a Renault 5 to be driven by JeanFrançois (who was arriving tomorrow).

JeanPaul and Annie would drive up to Tête Sauvage to recover Michel's car once we were underground, and take it to St. Engrâçe for our return.

Because the weight limitations on the plane had prevented us from bringing our own food and carbide, Michel had brought some for us. We all trooped out to the garage to fill our lamps and pack our tacklebags with the ample provisions that he had obtained. With all our preparations for the morning complete, Michel showed us up to the children's bedroom where we were to sleep in borrowed sleeping bags. Soon we were all fast asleep, the day's excitement counterbalanced by the wine and cognac.

At about 5 a.m. the phone rang and woke us all briefly. It was Jean-François confirming that he was en route! Sleep returned and we did not stir again until the bleeper on my watch sounded reveille at eight in the morning. We arose to a beautifully fresh and sunny morning. The Pyrenees looked as magnificent as ever and the air, cool and invigorating, ensured that we did not dawdle over our ablutions. Breakfast downstairs catered for all tastes...fruit juice, tea or coffee, rolls, eggs and cereals. We ate heartily and were still busy when JeanFrançois arrived with Jean, a tough looking Pyrenean carpenter and Gilles resplendent in a stripy tee-shirt, black beret and navy trousers. A general bustle ensued. The cars were soon loaded and we set off down the narrow roads twisting steeply down into the valley and up to the Pyrenees. Andy, Bill, JeanGilles and I travelled in Michel's old Peugeot, the rest in the Renault 5 belonging to JeanFrançois.

After about halfanhour's drive we came to the ski village of Arette La Pierre St.Martin. Here we left the metalled road and plunged on to a rocky, precipitous track. '*Affreux*' was Michel's description—and frightful it certainly was, in many places covered in large rocks which hit the underside of the car from time to time with the most expensive-sounding bangs and thuds. Michel revved the engine and fought the car along about two miles of this until we eventually reached the grassy hollow up on the top near the Tête Sauvage and pulled to a standstill near a parked car. Two cavers were sleeping on the ground and awoke on our arrival. They were from Carcassone and would do the detackling on Monday, but today they would follow behind us after a two or three hour interval. Michel explained the route to them and gave them a sketch map and then we started the ritual of changing into our caving gear.

Gilles had some new yellow gloves. He put these on his feet and strutted around like a chicken to the general amusement of us all. We all felt lighthearted and Bill and Andy started on the policeman jokes. I interpreted these for the benefit of the others and raised a laugh, too. Andy and I donned wetsuits, whilst the others put on thermal underwear and PVC oversuits. Whilst the French cavers carried spare clothes and rubber *pontonières* in their tackle bags, Bill carried his wetsuit, Andy took no spare clothes at all and I had a cotton overall and Damarts in sealed polythene bags. By now it was well after 10 a.m. and the sun was beating down so strongly that Andy and I began to sweat. Mercifully the entrance was only a short distance away, but it was a steep scramble uphill over the rocks in the full glare of the sun, so we were keen to enter the cool of the cave.

The Tête Sauvage entrance was easily recognised by a fifteen-foot wooden rectangular chimneylike construction used to keep the entrance clear of snow in the winter. JeanFrançois climbed up the outside clutching the guy ropes and standing precariously on minute projections afforded by the holding bolts. He disappeared inside, and since no one else appeared to be ready I followed. The climb up the outside of the wooden chimney was not too difficult, but the descent inside was obstructed by the Dexion framework holding the edifice together. My tackle bag, suspended by a cord from my sitharness, jammed and stuck, making my progress slow. I eventually dropped down into the rift below, however, and managed to sort things out.

The rift led to the first pitch, which was equipped with a fixed aid, called a *mât du perroquet* that literally translated means a parrot ladder. These aids were in place to a depth of around 200m. and each consisted of a tubular iron pole with rungs driven through at intervals of about 30cm. Since Michel had fixed safety lines, however, I clipped my rack in for protection and slid down the rungs hand over hand, my feet touching only when I needed to stop and see where I was going or to change from one rope to the next. The first pitch of about 10 metres led directly on to a 20m. pitch followed by a 30m. and then a 35m. pitch to the First Meander.

The First Meander was not too difficult to negotiate, but I had to crawl through the last part of it towing my tackle bag and then use my shoulders to wedge myself between the walls so that I could get on to the next pitch. This was a 70m. shaft equipped with four of the poles in series, the last one lying obliquely across the shaft and leading to an awkward constriction above a 20m. rope pitch. Here Andy came flying down with gay abandon and no attachments to the safety lines and overtook me. The bolt change on the other side of the constriction was quite awkward, involving a difficult move out over the 25m. drop below on a long cowstail, before I could take my weight on the short cowstail and attach my rack to the rope. I think Andy dispensed with these highassurance tactics and just hung on by his arms! The rope dropped me down to a large platform where I was narrowly missed by a pebble dislodged by Bill who had arrived at the constriction high above me. Several rope pitches followed down a steeply inclined rift dropping a further 50m. or so to another Meander.

The Second Meander was fairly easy and opened on to another rope pitch with a bolt change at a small ledge to the left. Unfortunately, there was insufficient slack in the rope for me to take out my rack from the first section. I had to hoist myself up bodily to release the rack, using my long cowstail for protection clipped into the bolt below...a most unsafe manoeuvre. As soon as the rack was free I managed to crab my short cowstail into the hanger and affect a conventional changeover. All of this faffing about allowed Bill time to catch up with me and I could hear the others hard on his heels, so I made a rapid descent to the Third Meander.

The Third Meander led to a series of easy climbs over large waterbasins, where I tried with some difficulty to keep my tackle bag dry. Here Bill decided to take a photograph of Andy who was now at the top of the final 100m shaft. Bill's camera was a doctored 'Instamatic' with a piece of string to hold the shutter open, the whole carried in a 1 litre lemonade bottle with the base cut off and stoppered with a waterproof plug. He hoped it would survive the trip! A great deal of shouting and flash bulb popping later, Andy departed downwards. Bill soon slid down the rope and it was my turn to follow.

The shaft was quite deep (over 100m.) and had been equipped with six bolt changes and a deflection belay to negotiate. Liaising between Bill below and Gilbert who was now above, called for a clear head not to mix the languages, as I could swear in both. The last bolt change was really entertaining and defied expletives in French or English. A large rib of rock stuck out from the opposite wall and the hanger for the final section of rope was inserted behind the rib, thus forcing one to swing out onto the rib somehow before being able to clip in and change ropes. A tatty piece of very ancient rope dangled off the rib and there were one or two tiny footholds on the rib itself. After a brief period of indecision, I swung out on the upper rope, clutched the rib, got a knee on the other side of it and grabbed the ancient rope. Muscles straining, and poised almost off balance on a negligible toehold, I managed to clip my cowstail into the Maillon on the last section and then dangled in an ungainly manner, struggling to undo my rack from the upper rope. Eventually I completed the changeover and made a smooth descent into a huge rift, where the lights of Andy, Bill and Jean-François were twinkling far below.

I soon found out why they were waiting: the next obstacle was a low duck. Bill decided that the overalls lent him by Michel had outlived their usefulness and that he would change into his wetsuit, whilst the others arrived. JeanFrançois lowered himself onto his back and slid under the duck, face upward to ensure an air supply. Andy and I followed face downwards and not too worried at the soaking as we were protected by our wetsuits.

The route continued down a series of climbs and two short pitches rigged with 8.5-mm cord. The area here was quite damp so I did not hang around, but even so, the other two were soon out of earshot. I found myself in a largish chamber and after climbing down a slanting slab and rift came to a streamway; presumably this was the Salle Cosyns although I could not be sure of that. With no sign of the other two I moved downstream, the roar of the water quite deafening as the passageway diminished. I took a right turn to avoid a deep pool and entered a narrow riftlike passage where my shouts were answered. Andy and JeanFrançois were sitting at the top of a calcite slope on the right-hand wall. On my own, I would never have seen the way on and I almost walked straight past them.

Whilst we waited for the others to arrive, I broke open a bar of chocolate from the supply in my helmet and as we munched, JeanFrançois explained the route ahead. So far we had been underground for only an hour and a half, so we were making good time. Eventually we heard a faint shout and Gilbert appeared below. Like me, he would have walked past, but for our shouts. The others trickled in behind, so we crawled through a small constriction and on to a climb down of about ten metres into another largish chamber, using a rope for safety and a spare figureofeight descender, as by now we had divested ourselves of all our SRT gear. On the other side we had to scramble up a steep slope leading to a large passageway, where we paused from a good vantage point to watch the others descend and cross the chamber, their lights outlining the route like cats' eyes. Bill tried to take a photograph and persuaded everyone to stand stock-still whilst he did so. By now his lemonade bottle was dented and decidedly fragile so I doubt if the shot was a success.

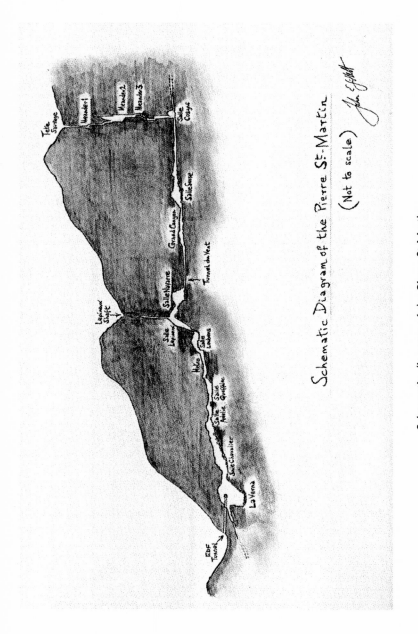

Schematic diagram of the Pierre St Martin

The way on was through a series of large, boulderstrewn passages where we made rapid progress to the 'Salle des Anciens,' a large dry chamber with a rubbish-strewn camping area. Here Michel called a halt for a snack and for the French cavers to put on their *pontonières* for the water ahead. By now, Bill and Andy had exhausted all of the 'policeman' jokes and were on to 'woman in bed' jokes. Gilles had finished his 'chicken' jokes and was on to 'sheep' jokes (when not inflating his *pontonière* to do a busty woman turn or two) so I reckoned that we must have been underground for about three hours or more.

Replete and all kitted out for watery routes, we set off once more at roughly the same level in high vaulted passageways strewn with boulders, following the occasional luminescent red waymarker as the route became more complex. At one point *(it may have been 'the Grande Corniche')* we had to inch across a narrow sloping slippery ledge, stooping to prevent our tackle bags fouling on the overhanging wall, with a bottomless pit on our left. Michel said that there used to be a fixed handline here once and I for one would have welcomed it. After this obstacle we scaled a small cliff, where a rocky foothold broke under my weight and I fell back on to my tackle bag several feet below. Luckily, I escaped unhurt. Then we got lost.

Michel and three others prusicked up a rope into some roof passages, but after a while concluded that this was the wrong route and so we all dispersed to look for way markers and the correct route ahead. By the time the correct passage had been found, we had occupied at least an hour or more in scouting operations. We dropped down into the water and waded and climbed various boulder falls until we entered the Grand Canyon, reminiscent of 'Go Faster' passage in Dan yr Ogof but much loftier. We marched along the pebblebedded streamway for over a kilometre, an exhilarating and most enjoyable part of our journey, until boulders blocked our progress again.

My memories of the exit from the Grand Canyon are vague, but we climbed up a 15m. pitch on an electron ladder that had been left in position as a fixed aid, to enter a smaller upper series of some complexity. We then came to another upward pitch rigged with an ancient piece of electron ladder with most of the rungs missing. Andy and JeanFrançois had quite a few problems in climbing up, as the hanger at the top was loose. The rest of us struggled up with the benefit of Andy holding the bolt down for us with his foot. Since this obstacle was timeconsuming, Bill took the opportunity for a nap. He had worked hard at the navigation during the flight and tiredness was beginning to catch up on him. We continued along a passage (which I recognised from Pierre Minvielle's book *The Hundred best trips in France*) with potholes filled with water to traverse or jump across. After several climbs, we eventually chimneyed down to the Canals.

Michel had been carrying a rubber dinghy for this eventuality and he soon had it unpacked and inflated. However, we wetsuited Britons had no need of such devices and explored ahead to find that we could keep dry above the waist by using handholds on the walls with only a modicum of floundering. This was good news for the French as they could keep dry in their *pontonières* and use the dinghy to ferry the tackle bags. Andy, Bill and I acted as ferrymasters and made good progress forwards until we came to the 'Tunnel of the Wind.'

Here the roof lowered and we had to unload half the bags to allow the dinghy to pass through. To add to our difficulties, the water became deeper and there was a sharp bend in the passage. Venturing onwards in the icy water, with a howling gale of such ferocity that our lamps blew out, we struggled with the dinghy using wire traverse lines in the roof to pull ourselves along.

After about a hundred yards, we came to a rocky island where we could see an enlargement ahead. Here we unloaded the tackle bags and Andy bravely set off through the tunnel towing the dinghy to collect the remainder, whilst Bill and I humped the first loads onto dry land in a massive chamber. Andy was soon back again with the rest of the bags. Then, even more heroically, he returned with the dinghy for the others to use as life support. We discovered that the *pontonières* were not so effective as buoyancy aids! Gilbert's *pontonière* let in water and he froze to the marrow; Gilles got a soaking, too, so our wetsuits proved to be the best investment.

We assembled on dry land and soon two gas stoves were roaring away beneath billies of water, whilst those who had dry clothes available changed into them. I opened my tackle bag, removed the polythene bags of dry Damarts and boiler suit, happily intact, and stripped off my wetsuit. Using the legs of the cotton boilersuit to dry myself, I soon warmed up and the final luxury of dry pants, Damart vest and longjohns was indescribable. A warm glow suffused my chilly limbs and once fully kitted out, my thoughts turned to food. Michel had provided enough sustenance for a siege! Whilst my 'Bolino' macaroni and mince cooked, I ate some cheese, pâté and nuts, washed down with lemonade. The hot 'Bolino' was delicious and after polishing it all off I helped Gilbert finish his soup. With chocolate and dried fruit to follow, it was a veritable banquet. Anyway, it filled the energy gap of nine or ten hours continuous caving.

The changing, cooking and feasting took some time and everyone perked up, although Bill and Andy, who had no dry clothes to change into, were shivering uncomfortably at the end. They were glad when our caravanserai moved on again. The galleries following were of the enormous dimensions normally associated with the PSM and we soon heated up with the exercise of rapid walking and scrambling on the trail of the red routemarkers. Soon a rope pitch upwards confronted us. Using ascenders for protection we free climbed, hauling the tackle bags after us. I ascended last and of course the final tackle bags jammed, so I had to use up precious energy to descend and retrieve them. We were now in the complex of the Salle Navarre, where Michel navigated adroitly so that in a short time we were at the top of the rubble heap below the Lepineux shaft.

It was four years since I had visited this region of the cave and as I slithered down the scree slope towards Louben's tomb, I noticed that Michel and Gilbert were standing exactly where I had photographed them all that time ago. The timeless atmosphere was unchanged and the smoky lettering on the now empty tomb still proclaimed its eternal message. I had that eerie feeling of *déja vu* and wondered if I was destined ever to pass this way again. My reverie was broken by the general movement and bustle of our group towards the exit.

The next section was through an enormous boulder ruckle, equipped with a handline to avoid the dangerously loose areas. We had to go through a small hole between ominously poised boulders that required a firm hold on the rope to avoid clutching a catastrophe. One by one we carefully lowered ourselves through the blocks and filed along the Elizabeth Casteret chamber and on into the Loubens cave.

By now, although our tackle bags were biting into our shoulders and our legs becoming leaden, we were on familiar ground and made good progress so that we were soon in the vast gallery of the Metro. We took the left-hand wall with the torrent on our right and, after a short pause to regroup, marched on along a wellbeaten track and then on over the boulders into the Queffelec Chamber. Here Michel, Bill and I, who were in the rear, took a wrong turn leading to a high route where we temporarily lost sight of the others. We eventually regained the main route, however, and caught them up as they were crawling over the ledge past the large pool guarding the Salle Chevalier.

The Salle Chevalier is indescribably enormous and as we traversed along the right hand wall we were awed by its grandeur. Our path lay along a series of narrow ledges, very loose in places with a steep, occasionally vertical drop to the stream below. As we progressed along the chamber, the stream became lost in the deep blackness below us and eventually we reached a constriction caused by a boulderfall, where we had to take off our packs and crawl.

We emerged into the monstrous blackness of La Verna, the largest underground cavity in the Western World. In several places we stopped to gaze into the void, to try to pick out the Aranzadi Wall on the other side, but we were falling behind and had to keep moving. Soon we reached the EDF tunnel, easily located by a fenced pathway and steps above the yawning abyss. The tunnel cut by the EDF still had railway lines in it and Bill tried to balance on these to keep his feet dry, as he had no other shoes to wear. In places the roof timbers were in a state of collapse. In one place Bill trod in a deep puddle with resultant expletives sufficient to trigger a complete roof failure. However, the mundane tunnels soon ended and before long we stood before the final doors, deafened by the wind roaring out through the cracks. As we edged through, the wind blew us out into the midnight air.

In the cabin near the entrance we could see the flicker of firelight, and—could we believe it? —smell cooking! Two heroes of the Ziloko, man and wife, had driven up to the cabin, lit a log fire, and cooked soup for us. What comradeship! We sat ourselves down on the wooden benches and slurped up the hot chicken noodle soup so generously provided, as our legs tingled with relief after the long traverse. Bill found an old mattress in the corner and fell asleep. A brief rest and some desultory conversation and then the final walk to St. Engrâce had to be faced. I knew that it would take at least an hour, from previous experience, and that was in daylight. Bill could not be roused, so Andy, JeanFrançois and I started off downhill, leaving the others to get their boots back on and drag Bill out of bed.

The route downhill was along a wellworn track and we passed the van used by the Ziloko members who had lit the fire for us. My lamp suddenly went out, and in fixing it I fell behind the other two who were moving at a fast pace. From then on I failed to catch up with them but trudged on as fast as I could, catching a glimpse of their lights as the track twisted and turned along the hillside and in amongst the trees. As we neared St. Engrâce I shouted to them, as I knew a shortcut which branched off directly down through the scrubby open ground at the bottom of the hill. They waited for me and we stumbled downhill until we reached the stream with a wooden bridge over it, that I recognised from a previous visit. Soon we were on the metalled road leading up to St. Engrâce and we found Michel's car parked in a lay-by at the bottom of the steep hill.

Peering through the windows we could see our dry clothes, toilet gear and sleeping bags inside, but search as we might it was impossible to find the key and gain access to them. We decided to carry on up to the *Gite d'Etape* in the village and wait there for Michel. Once more our legs were goaded into action, but mine would not go as well as those of Andy and JeanFrançois and halfway up I just had to stop and sit down. A few minutes' rest and I felt slightly refreshed (we had been walking on the surface for over an hour now) and made my way steadily up to the village, where the lights were on in the bunkhouse and I could see Andy sitting in the porch.

Outside the hotel was a tap, and so thirsty was I that I turned it on and took the full bore in my mouth, regardless of potential tummy bugs from the large slug hunched on the pipe below. We had caused something of a commotion, as there seemed to be a busload of schoolgirls inside and their giggling and chattering seemed quite incongruous. Luckily, our bunks were upstairs. Andy and I sat and waited and soon the van appeared bearing Bill, who had cadged a lift downhill, followed shortly by Michel with our clothes. Hot showers were available, so we could now remove the last of our sweaty clothes and clean ourselves up. With little ceremony we all found bunkspace and were soon fast asleep in our sleeping bags, oblivious to the world for a while.

No one stirred until at least 9 a.m., and then we went to the bar next door to buy breakfast. I was amazed to find that I was not at all stiff, especially as my legs had felt so tired at the end, but maybe summer in the Jura had given me more stamina than I thought possible. *Café complet* came and we sat around the tables on the terrace outside the bar, just across the road from the squat Pyrenean church, eating rolls and jam whilst the conversation flowed. Our traverse had taken about 14 hours altogether and we exchanged views on the various events that had taken place. Believe it or not, we actually started to plan what to do next summer! JeanFrançois had traversed the Reseau Trombe, which was my next target, and we started to discuss possibilities. The time flashed past and we were suddenly reminded that if we wanted to get back to Biggin Hill, we should leave *dés que possible*.

Our farewells took some time as only JeanGilles was coming back with us in Michel's car, and we would not see the others for several years, if ever again. Our companionship and common bond had forged a wellknit team and the camaraderie that had developed was a pleasure not to be relinquished easily.

Bags packed, boots closed, we shut the car doors and, narrowly missing several chickens, drove off en route for Issor. On we went, Michel and me speaking French in the front with cross talk to JeanGilles and a mixture from Andy and Bill in the back. Soon we swept up the hill and on to the drive of Michel's house.

Annie had prepared an excellent lunch for us and once again we were overwhelmed by her French hospitality. Before we could eat, however, out came the bathroom scales and Bill weighed himself, Andy, Ron, and me and all of our gear. I think I had put on weight! Ron and Bill were rather concerned about the short bumpy runway at Oloron and did lots of calculations on fag packets and chocolate wrappers. The rest of us sat down to lunch, facing the view across the Pyrenees and somewhat sad at our imminent departure. We had to go at last and Michel helped us to load the car for the final ride to the airstrip. We said goodbye to Annie and the children, to JeanPaul and his family, and to JeanGilles, then Michel drove us away down the steep Pyrenean lanes to our waiting aeroplane. Flight checks completed, Ron discovered that the fuel tanks were nearly empty so we should be O.K. for lift-off provided we could make a fuel stop soon. Once again, our tiny plane clawed its way into the sky and after a circle to wave goodbye to Michel, Ron set course for Pau airport using the navigation beacons on automatic direction finding. After all our physical and emotional exercise, here we were once more encased in modern technology.

Our landing and refuelling at Pau was trouble free and, with a good tail wind, we reached Deauville in three hours, Andy and I drowsing in the back for most of the way. On the ground we bought our duty frees, refuelled and had afternoon tea before takeoff. Soon we were airborne again, over the Channel, and in a remarkably short time, landing at Biggin Hill in a welter of Sunday fliers.

The English Customs were quite meticulous. Our plane was emptied of bags and inspected, and they looked in our tackle bags. My stinking wetsuit was sufficiently repellent, however, to prevent a complete unpacking. Tired and slightly dazed by our activities, we strolled into the bar for a few beers and for Ron to complete his flight log. Our trip to the Pyrenees was over as quickly as it had begun.

18

Canyon de Sadum

The Pyrenees always seem to be full of surprises, and my visit there in the summer of 1986 proved no exception. Michel, an old caving friend, had invited us to stay in his house, high on the hill overlooking the village of Issor. We arrived late in the afternoon after a hot and tiring drive from a caving expedition in Spain, to a most hospitable welcome from Michel and Annie his wife. Soon we were sitting on the lawn with the magnificent panorama of the Pyrenees before us and cool drinks in our hands. It was not long before *'La Spéléologie'* was mentioned. Michel revealed that there was the first descent of a local canyon planned for the morrow. It meant a very early start, or alternatively there was a recently discovered cave to explore through a six-metre long sump. I hate sumps and felt like a lie-in, so toyed with the idea of a day sunbathing, but reason prevailed and I opted for the canyon.

We rose at five a.m., ate a substantial breakfast and drove off into the darkness at a seemingly incredible speed, eventually taking the road for the Col du Sompfort. At about six a.m. we drove up a rough track behind the village of Etsaut and, passing two cars left by the canyon team the night before, pulled up in a quarried lay-by. It was still pitch dark, which made changing difficult. Since we had a two and a half-hour walk uphill before us, I put my wetsuit, descending gear and rope into my tackle bag and limited my clothing to boots, underpants and a tee shirt. Michel had packed a prodigious amount of food for the expedition that we shared between us, so our sacks were rather heavy. A quick look at the map in torchlight and we took an obvious patch into the trees, disturbing a grumpy badger at his nocturnal foraging.

The path was well made and we strode along it until suddenly we were confronted by a barrier well laced with barbed wire and surmounted by a sign threatening trespassers with a backside of buckshot. Impasse! Michel consulted the map. A dog howled in the nearby farmstead, but no one seemed to be awake, so after throwing our tackle over the barrier, we crawled through a hole in the hedge and continued uphill.

The path soon became overgrown. Nettles and briars raked our bare legs. The path became steeper, more arduous and after an hour's uphill grind we emerged from the woods on to the side of a mountain. Michel consulted the map again and asked my advice, but without spectacles I was of no help. We climbed higher to obtain a better view. The canyon could now be seen in the next valley! There was nothing for it but to descend and traverse around the hillside to gain the correct path. After half an hour's rapid movement, we eventually found the Scotch-tape left for us by the canyon team. They had ascended to the Pas d' Ourtasse the previous evening and camped out for an eight a.m. start.

By now it was seven thirty a.m. and obvious that we could no longer make the rendezvous, so we climbed uphill until about nine o'clock and then searched for a way down into the canyon so that we could intercept them. Luckily we found a place where it was possible to climb down into the ravine without ropes, so that if we missed the descending team, we could still climb back out of the canyon later.

The water in the bottom was at its summer low, but even so was flowing in a fair volume and as we progressed upstream, each waterfall presented a serious obstacle. We managed to climb several waterfalls and to clamber over log and boulder piles in the streambed, until finally we came to a waterfall that was over ten metres high and defied our efforts to ascend. Here we decided to wait for the others. After changing into my wetsuit, I lay down, quite exhausted and went to sleep.

I awoke in bright sunlight that had penetrated the ravine, roused by a call from above. It was JeanClaude, an extremely fit and agile rock climber, the discoverer of the canyon. He was leading Coco and Pasquale who were cavers from the same club as Michel. They were all in their twenties, full of energy and enthusiasm and well hung with rope and climbing equipment. A spell of hammering to fix bolts and they abseiled down to join us.

We discussed what had happened. So far, they had been in the canyon for three hours and at one point had had to descend a cascade that was forty metres deep using two of their ropes knotted together. None of us knew what obstacles we would find lower down...I hoped that we had enough bolts and attachments between us and that we would encounter no falls over the depth of our longest rope. Although Jean-Claude seemed to have an inexhaustible supply of tape and hangers in his sack our ropes could still limit us, especially if the longest one became irretrievably stuck on a rappel. JeanClaude, Coco and Pasquale were all in high spirits and anxious to continue the descent as there were still several kilometres of the canyon to complete. Off they went, leaving Michel and me to struggle into our harnesses.

We eventually caught up with them about a hundred metres downstream of the place where we had climbed down into the ravine earlier in the morning. Here they were busy fixing bolts for the descent of a twenty metres deep fall. The descent was accomplished without getting wet and when we were all at the bottom the rope was pulled down without snagging. Around the next corner we came to a couple of spray-lashed five-metre deep falls in a narrow rift. A long slide followed, descended in the sitting position, and from then on I lost count of the descents; but we encountered several deep pools at the base of one or two of them that made retrieval of the ropes difficult.

Since I was the last in line, my job was to pull down the ropes, which I did until they ran out of rope at the front or until I became overladen. The top of each waterfall always allowed us to regroup and whilst the bolts were driven in, we could look down to assess the route and try to guess what the next curve or spumemisted gorge would reveal. The excitement of not knowing what was around the next corner was most exhilarating. At one point we encountered a deep waterfall which plummeted into a dark cleft in which it was impossible to see the bottom for spray. The noise of the water here was deafening and we could barely hear each other. I was the first to descend here and as I slid off into the steaming abyss I prayed that the rope was long enough to reach the bottom.

Engulfed in spray and buffeted by the wind of the falling water I became lost to sight. Luckily there was a small sloping ledge for me to pause on just in time to discover that there was a deep pool further below. I made a cautious descent into this until I could find an underwater shelf to stand on. Once off the rope it was difficult to communicate with the others, but by pulling on the rope and blowing on my whistle I managed to convince them that I had landed safely so that they could join me.

Several of the falls were technically difficult. One cascade was just like the last pitch of Diccan Pot in Yorkshire, only a bit deeper. Another jetted off a large shelf which overhung the canyon to provide a superb free-hang; yet another was down an enclosed rift with the water ricocheting from side to side between the walls. I had never realised what sport a canyon could provide! In spite of the realisation that we could not retrace our steps and that we must continue our descent to escape the confines of the canyon, we all felt confident that we could overcome whatever obstacles we met.

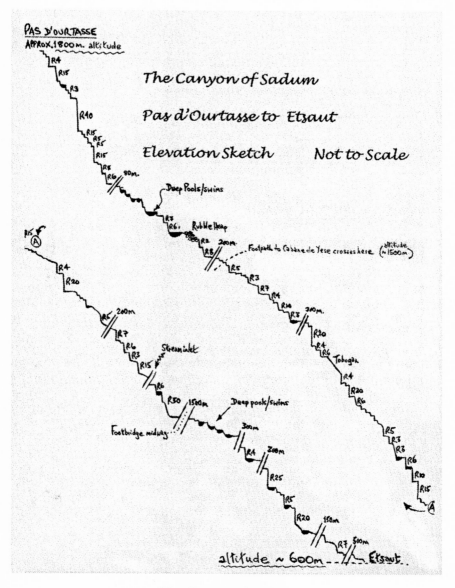

The Canyon of Sadum

Soon our breathtaking descent petered out into a long tiring section of jungly fallen branches and massive boulders where the gradient was less steep. Bringing up the rear, Pasquale and I began to lag behind; we seemed to be carrying too much tackle and this made many of the obstacles hard to negotiate. One of the coiled ropes that I was carrying began to work loose and snag on the branches as if it had a will of its own. My helmet caught in a low branch, I started to sweat and become irritated, especially when the others shouted to us to get a move on. Fortunately the route passed beneath a small footbridge where it was decided to stop for a snack. By now it was mid afternoon and I had been on the go for over nine hours. How pleasant it was to divest myself of the wretched ropes and tacklebags and to sit down unencumbered!

Our rest stop was, however, over too soon for me. Feeling distinctly middleaged, I found it hard to restart, but luckily around the next corner we came to several invigoratingly cold pools, some of which were very deep. Because the walls of the canyon were sheer at this point, we had to swim in places for quite a long distance. Unfortunately my heavy tackle bag threatened to drown me! I had forgotten to re-tie the contents in their polythene bag after the rest stop. Lacking the essential buoyancy as I swam along, I was gradually being pulled under. Even on the point of drowning I refused to release the bag, as its contents were valuable and essential to my ultimate survival. A difficult decision! Luckily Michel came to my rescue and with a little help I was saved from a watery grave.

A further tree-infested section of low gradient followed until we reached a cascade about twenty-five metres deep into a wide pool that looked green and bottomless. This required a most hairraising descent, blindly immersed in falling water, aiming for a jammed log at the bottom to stand on in order to unclip from the rope. A few more cascades and pools followed and it was not long before we were in the village of Etsaut and able to climb out into the square, now bathed in hot afternoon sunshine. Still clad in our wetsuits, we walked straight to the village bar and JeanClaude ordered drinks. Exhilaration overcame our tiredness and we toasted the first descent of the Canyon of Sadum, twelve hundred metres from top to bottom and over five kilometres long.

Since the first descent, the canyon has been closed for conservation reasons. It was subsequently discovered that the canyon was the habitat of a family of rare Pyrenean bears. They obviously hid from us on the day of our descent, probably in the area where Michel and I fell asleep! They must have been as aware of our presence that day as we were unaware of theirs!

19

Les Manants

April, and three months of extremely hard and stressful work drew to a final close midday on a Friday. A snack lunch on cheese and tomato baps and we drove off down the motorways to Coldred in Kent for dinner in the local pub and a night under the eaves of an ancient farmhouse. Up at the crack of dawn and off on the Hovercraft for a bumpy crossing to Calais. At a steady hundred and forty kilometres an hour, we slid down the autoroutes, got lost at Lille and arrived at Liege, lost again and late for our rendezvous.

Janine, who happened to be passing, saw our car by the phone box from which we were telephoning for help. She rescued us and took us through a maze of streets to the house of Alphonse and Yvonne. A pleasant lunch followed in a babble of conversation, and then we travelled across town again and moved into the attic of Pierre and Janine's house in the Faubourg Sainte Gilles. Six flights of steep stairs repeated with loads of baggage warmed us up as we installed ourselves at roof level. After a tour of the house, we returned for a barbecue and Belgian beer until the early hours of the morning. To bed at last and out like a light.

I rose early to be treated to a large cooked breakfast. Janine had prepared a large pan full of eggs and bacon especially for me. There was just time to eat it and then we climbed aboard Pierre's Range Rover and drove off with Alphonse and Laurent to the nearby hills for a descent of the pothole of Les Manants. This swallet, recently discovered by Alphonse and Pierre, was a key part of a major local caving system. At the roadhead, we changed into dry gear, buckled on our harnesses and equipment and then walked through the woods, the trees still bare and waiting to bud. We were soon at the cave entrance near the sink of a small and smelly stream.

The entrance looked dangerously loose and muddy to me. Alphonse climbed down through the boulders into the entrance shaft over slippery wooden stemples placed at random to prevent a total collapse. I followed, my gear snagging on projections and at the bottom soon became stuck in the small orifice that had originally been dug out by Pierre and Alphonse. I soon realised that it was a mistake to descend such a constricted entrance fully equipped, as each successive squeeze and wriggle became more arduous. Eventually we came to a small chamber where I could stand up and sort myself out.

By now my electric cell was loose around my waist and my climbing gear a muddy lump of cord and alloy dangling between my legs. Alphonse, slim as a rake, slithered off down another muddy slot and I forced and struggled after him. So far, I had passed all that the cave had to offer and I began to wonder why they had warned me that the cave was tight. Alphonse seemed to be having a bit of difficulty ahead, but soon dropped out of sight down a vertical constricted hole. *"C'est un peu étroit,"* he said laconically.

I looked at the problem and decided that, with my bad back, I should enter the vertical squeeze feet first and facing the opposite direction to that which Alphonse had used. As I sank up to my chest in the slot, I jammed solid. No movement at all! I squirmed and wriggled, but it was obvious that my climbing gear and electric cell had to come off. I withdrew to a larger cavity where it was just possible to undo the buckles and shackles and allowed Pierre to pass me. I knew he was in for trouble for he was slightly larger than I was, although he had passed the constriction on a previous occasion. I could hear him grunting and struggling and soon, divested of encumbrances, I was back at the construction to observe his progress. Pierre seemed to be completely jammed and red in the face with his exertions. *"Hissez, hissez!"* he shouted to Alphonse who was trying to assist him from below. Alphonse obliged and Pierre's chest grated as he forced through; at least his blood would lubricate my efforts! The "Yang" approach of muscle and determination obviously worked.

I entered the slot cautiously, feeling its shape with my hips and thighs, sinking in gradually until my chest became jammed. I turned slowly to try and find the widest possible section, but I was stuck on bone in two places. I withdrew to seek a better position. Three further attempts almost convinced me that I could not pass, but I knew that Pierre's chest was bigger than mine and so logically I should be able to get through, even if I was less supple. I decided on one final attempt. Wriggling and relaxing I slid down until Alphonse and Pierre could direct my feet. Laurent took my cell and gear and I concentrated on getting my chest into the widest part of the constriction. A final shove, exhaling, and I slid through, scraping my breastbone only slightly. Success!

According to Alphonse, that was the tightest bit, so I felt confident that I could continue. Laurent followed easily and then we had to squirm through a couple of tight Sbends and into a further horizontal section. I soon developed a way of heaving my cell and gear separately so that I could pass the tight sections relatively easily. Eventually we came to a chamber where we could stand up.

To exit the chamber we had to climb up into the roof and so I had to reassemble and put on my harnesses for the ascent of a rope. The climb was quite straightforward and led into further muddy tubes of less intimidating smallness than those in the entrance series. Eventually we came to a steep slippery descent ending at a small ledge over a fifteen-metre pitch. Alphonse descended and I soon followed, to land in a muddy chamber where other members of the club on a separate trip were waiting to greet us. Pierre and Laurent descended to join us and then we had to continue up a short climb to a narrow descending fissure.

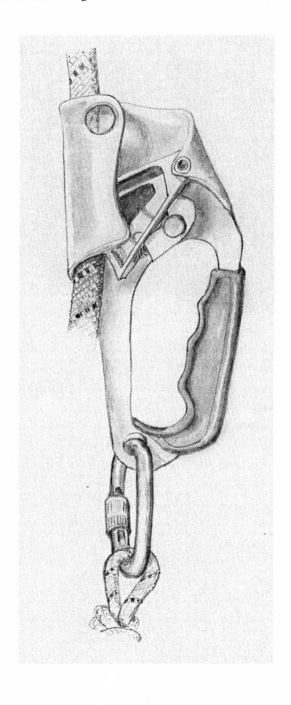

The fissure looked very intimidating but Alphonse passed through fairly easily. I tried to follow him but soon became well and truly stuck. Suddenly I realised that I was quite exhausted. After a few feeble struggles, I decided to return to the chamber and rest for a while. I felt absolutely weak, my arms and legs had no strength in them, the muscles useless.

In the chamber I sat against the wall, tired out and completely drained of energy. I really felt that something was wrong with me and the thought that Pierre was an internationally famous cardiologist did little to dispel my fears. For the first time I felt my age. The thought of never being able to go caving again flashed across my mind. A depression set in. I'll never go to Cueto Coventosa! I'll have to be rescued! Misery, despair! Closing my eyes, I relaxed completely and concentrated on steady breathing. I told myself that I was an experienced caver who could get to the surface and that my energy would return. Unfortunately I had no sweets or chocolate, it was only a short trip, or I would have eaten something. I revived a little and decided to return the way that we had come.

Pierre, who had by now passed the constriction, shouted for me to follow. I told him that I had no energy and that I wanted to go back the way that I had come. Pierre and Alphonse shouted for me to come through as that would be the quickest way out and that the fissure was easy. I somehow managed to climb up to the entrance to the fissure, but once there I still felt very weak and useless. I inserted my feet into the fissure and shouted to Pierre and Alphonse that I would try again. They promised to catch me as I came through. (They were now in a small chamber a few metres below). Trusting entirely in Pierre and Alphonse, I slid into the fissure, utterly relaxed, with all my muscles loose, floppy like a half-empty sack. Like magic, I oozed through under gravity, just managing to grab a small handhold to stop my full weight falling on my comrades below. I was through!

Laurent followed without much difficulty and we made our way down to a waterfall in a busy streamway. I still felt weak and had to sit down again to recover. I think in retrospect it was a case of utter exhaustion, more mental than physical, due to the late nights and travelling exacerbated by low blood sugar level, but in any case I managed to revive at last.

Our route back to the surface involved the ascent of a couple of rope pitches, so I started out with Alphonse whilst Pierre and Laurent continued downstream to the sump to collect some equipment that they had left there. I managed to ascend the pitches with no difficulty and also the succeeding climbs and crawls. Soon we were back at the infamous squeeze. I passed this upwards with very little trouble, probably because I had explored its contours and intimate details so well on the way in.

In no time at all I was back on the surface, completely covered with mud, my cell and equipment a muddy bundle and my eyes blinking in the bright sunshine. Our little trip had taken about four hours, but to me one part of it seemed to have lasted a lifetime!

20

Troglodytes

It is amazing how humanity has advanced in the relatively short time since its emergence. Astrophysicists have estimated that the universe was formed about fifteen billion years ago and the Earth more than four billion years ago. Such enormous numbers are bread and butter to astrophysicists, but the rest of us, who sometimes cannot remember what happened last week, find them incomprehensible. A million years is a long while, but a billion seems like eternity. Nevertheless, time has passed and the events that happened in past millennia still have an impact on our lives. For example, the limestones containing caves were formed about three hundred million years ago and the last glaciation ended about twenty-two thousand years ago. These significant events for caving were very deep in the past, especially against the standards of 2000 AD with its puny 'Millennium' celebrations. In the history of the planet one thousand years is just a moment.

The first true humans began their lives at the end of the last glaciation, but there were several hominids that existed well before that. The earliest tool-maker was probably *Australopithecus Africanus* who lived about two million years ago. *Homo sapiens* evolved from these ape-like hominids through various stages to the present day. The last of the ape-men were the Neanderthal who lived about 40–100,000 years ago and were replaced by the Cro-Magnon, the first true men. Of these, the Magdalenian culture that existed about 20,000 years ago, with its fine tools and cave paintings, was the most advanced.

All of these early hominids and humans used natural caves for shelter. In some cases their caves were subsequently blocked or the entrances collapsed, protecting them from further use or destruction. The discovery and excavation of such caves provided a rich source of information to archaeologists and an occasional amazing find for cave explorers.

My own interest in cave archaeology was very superficial and based on learning about 'The Stone Age' at school supplemented by sparse information from caving books. However, when I was working at the University of the Witwatersrand in Johannesburg I had an opportunity to learn more. I knew that the Sterkfontein cave, where *Australopithecus Africanus* was discovered, was only fifty kilometres away and planned to visit it. Giles, who was working with me, knew the area well and, although he had never been there, was keen to try something different. He was easily persuaded to drive me there. We set off into the Transvaal, aiming for the region near Krugersdorp. Giles avoided the main roads. He wanted me to experience the countryside better. Soon after leaving Johannesburg, we left the tarmac roads for the bush. We drove several kilometres on dirt tracks across an immense dry plain. In front of us were wide blue skies and a distant horizon, behind us a pall of dust from our tyres. Occasional small trees and bushes decorated an arid, fairly desolate landscape that had an orange hue. There were few signs of life, but I distinctly remember Giles swerving to avoid a very large snake in our path. In the middle of nowhere, we passed two native people walking along the track and slowed down to avoid dusting them. They smiled and waved to us as we passed. Judging by the state of the surface, cars were a rare sight on this track. The hire car took quite a beating over the bumps and rocks, as did we! Our destination proved to be worth it, however.

We arrived to find that Sterkfontein Caves had been developed as a tourist attraction. The site was on a small hill with a panoramic view of the plain. We could see that there was a tarmac access road from a national highway for tourists, a good car park, a small restaurant and

an informative museum. We seemed to have arrived off peak, as there
were only five cars in the car park. Giles and I bought tickets for a
guided tour of the caves. As we waited for the guide to arrive, we
inspected the current excavations in the breccia nearby. They occupied
a considerable surface area and were arrayed with scaffolding and wires
that divided the site into individual plots for archaeological studies.
The site had been a rich source of hominid fossils and tools since it was
first dug at the end of the nineteenth century. The most famous finds
were of *Australopithecus Africanus*, a key link between apes and
humans.

The guide eventually arrived with half a dozen other visitors. After a
short talk in the scorching heat, he led us into the cave. The entrance
was about a hundred metres from the latest excavations. We stooped
under a low arch and went down a flight of steps into a deep, narrow
rift. At the bottom we followed a narrow path until the rift opened into
a natural cave. The cool atmosphere was a welcome respite from the
hot plain overhead. The guide stopped by a plaque to 'Mrs. Ples' whose
skull had been found in the cave in 1947. According to the archeolo-
gists, she lived about two million years ago. He told us of the skull's
history and of how it had convinced scientists that *Australopithecus
Africanus* should be included in the family tree of modern humans. He
also explained the geology and history of the cave in simple terms,
stimulating many questions from the other visitors.

When he was satisfied that he had answered all of the questions, the
guide led us further into the cave. The passage was quite narrow and at
one point there was an aven that gave us a glimpse of daylight high
above. We had to stoop to pass through a low constriction and to
weave around boulders to reach a more spacious area. Here, there were
formations on the cave walls and lumpy stalactites in the roof in some
places. It was a proper cave! The guide, needless to say, had names for
the various obstacles and chambers that we encountered. I remember
that the largest chamber was called 'The Hall of the Elephants' and the
stooping section 'Lumbago Alley.' The final chamber, about sixty

metres below the surface, contained an underground lake. We all stood in silence, impressed by the stillness of the surface and the limpid water. Although it was unlikely that *Australopithecus* ever saw it, the lake was a thought-provoking ending to our visit. As we slowly made our way out of the cave, my imagination filled in the gaps between now and the distant past of the ape-men. I wondered what they looked like and if they thought of anything except food. It seemed incredible that our genes could contain sections of code from them. Giles was quite sure that they were our forefathers. According to him, one of his colleagues was a proper monkey!

On reflection, I thought that Sterkfontein was more interesting to me as a natural cave than as a visual proof of our ancestor's existence. In such matters one can only trust the experience and knowledge of the archaeologists. The caves inhabited by later cultures such as the Magdalenian and Neolithic provide more visually interesting and exciting material than those inhabited by ape-men. Magdalenian tools and paintings are beautifully made and reveal that they were as artistic and intelligent as we are. Two such sites that I have visited spring to mind, the El Buxu cave in the Picos de Europa and the Tito Bustillo cave on the Costa Verde.

Although I had only a superficial interest in prehistoric art, I was very impressed by the tales of some of my caving friends who had found artifacts and paintings during their exploration of local caves. Cave preservation authorities usually sealed such discoveries quickly to prevent damage so I was never able to see them myself. My first opportunity to see real prehistoric art was when Catherine and I were camping in the farmyard behind the bar Germán with the annual Matienzo expedition. We were told that there were prehistoric drawings in a small cave on the way up the valley. Several cavers claimed to have seen them although others said that they were difficult to find. We took the best advice available and climbed up to the cave. However, we were disappointed. Search the walls as we might, we saw nothing. So it was not until I went to the Picos de Europa on a walking holiday with Dilys, that I saw a real prehistoric drawing for the first time.

We were staying in a hotel in Las Arenas and were planning a tour to Covadonga and lakes Enol and Ercina. I noticed that the Michelin guide to Spain that I was using mentioned a cave called El Buxu that contained some Magdalenian drawings and engravings that was just off our route. We decided to visit it. However, on the ground it was not easy to find. After almost giving up, we eventually asked the way at a garage near Cangas de Onis. In those days, my Spanish was rather limited, but I knew the difference between *derecha* and *izquierda*. I was thus able to follow the directions of the garage attendant, do a U-turn and take a small track to the left of the main road down which we had just driven. We parked the car at the end of the rough track lined with trees and overgrown bushes and walked up to a cottage. There was a cliff face nearby that presumably contained the cave. A woman clad in a black dress was working in the garden. She spoke no English, but I managed to explain that we wanted to visit the cave. She took a few pesetas for the entry fee and went into the cottage. A few minutes later, she emerged wearing an old shawl and carrying a hand torch. We followed her along a path to the cave entrance and entered the cave. It was damp and musty inside, but relatively dry underfoot. She turned on her torch and we stumbled along behind her into the darkness, keeping our heads down to avoid hitting them on the ceiling. I cannot remember exactly, but it was not very far before she stopped to shine the light on the wall. At first we could see nothing, then peering closely in the pale light of the torch, it was possible to see an engraving of a horse. It was only about the size of a hand, but exquisitely drawn with smooth flowing lines. The artist had skillfully and precisely captured the animal's movement. All that I can remember is the horse in the pitch darkness. The rest of the cave vanished as I concentrated on the image before me. It was so unexpectedly beautiful that I held my breath. Our guide did not move, nor did we. It was a timeless moment.

The rest of the tour was more mundane as we tried to make out faint charcoal drawings, lines and smoke marks left by the Magdalenians countless years ago. As we left for Covadonga, I could not help thinking that although El Buxu was a few hundred miles from the Reina Sofia in Madrid, the artistry of its horse was no less than that of the one in Picasso's Guernica. Across thousands of years the animals had changed little nor had the artistry.

A few years later, Dilys and I were making a leisurely pilgrimage to Santiago de Compostela, exploring the Costa Verde en route. After disembarking from the Santander ferry we did not want to drive too far and decided to spend a few nights in a hotel in Ribadesella before continuing our journey westward. The receptionist in the hotel was most welcoming and helpful and, during our conversation, she told us about the local show cave. I had tried several times to obtain access to the famous Altemira caves with no success. It seemed to me that the cave preservation was so important that visitors were kept as far from the real paintings as possible. As a consequence, I had never visited any of the renowned painted caves. In Ribadesella, however, we struck lucky.

Not only did we see some beautiful cave paintings close at hand, but we were given a free tour into the bargain.

According to our trusty Michelin Guide, the Tito Bustillo show cave contained some beautiful Magdalenian wall paintings of stags and horses coloured with red or ochre about a quarter of a mile inside a natural cave. Dilys and I made our visit with four Spanish tourists. The guide, who spoke little English, led us through the cave with a commentary in Spanish that I was able to interpret for Dilys. When we arrived at the paintings, she allowed us plenty of time to look at them. The lighting was well concealed and illuminated the colours and engraved outlines without being too strong to dispel the feeling of age and mystery. One could image all sorts of ghosts lurking in the shadows. Once the guide had finished her story, the silence was palpable. No one spoke. All of us were immersed in our own thoughts. The animals seemed to glow as if their creators had endowed them with their own magic. It was the guide who eventually broke our reverie. She had seen them all many times and wanted to get on with her day's work. We were reluctantly led away and back to the entrance, carrying vivid images in our memories.

Whenever I think of the artistry and elegance of the cave paintings and engravings that I have seen I cannot help thinking that we are no different from the people who made them. In spite of our advanced education and technological knowledge, we are still essentially similar physically and mentally even though there are tens of thousands of years between us. In the enormous time since the planet was formed mankind has advanced with incredible speed during its brief spell of existence. Considering that it took billions of years before the ape-men evolved and then tens of thousands more for them to evolve into humans, what on earth are we evolving into ourselves? Will we become hybrids connected to machines? Are there already beings among us who have evolved as yet unknown abilities? Will we create a new species ourselves using genetic engineering? What kind of cavers will the next ten thousand years bring?

21

Sima Cueto to Coventosa

The *Quiberon* slid smoothly across the Bay of Biscay on a calm sea. Keith, Jenny, Catherine and I sat in the bar idly sipping our drinks and gazing at the sunlit sea. It was Wednesday. Next Tuesday, Keith and I would start one of the most beautiful and sporting subterranean traverses in the world. The traverse from the deep shafts of Sima Cueto via several kilometres of galleries to the beautiful lakes and final porch of the Coventosa cave.

A year ago, whilst caving with us in Britain, our friends of the Club de Recherches Spéléologiques de Liege had invited us on their expedition to traverse Cueto Coventosa. They planned to camp near Santander on a site at Soma beach. We, however, decided to camp free and rough at Matienzo as it was within half an hour of the Coventosa entrance and we had used it before. The final plans would be discussed on Sunday at the Belgians' campsite, where we looked forward to renewing old acquaintances.

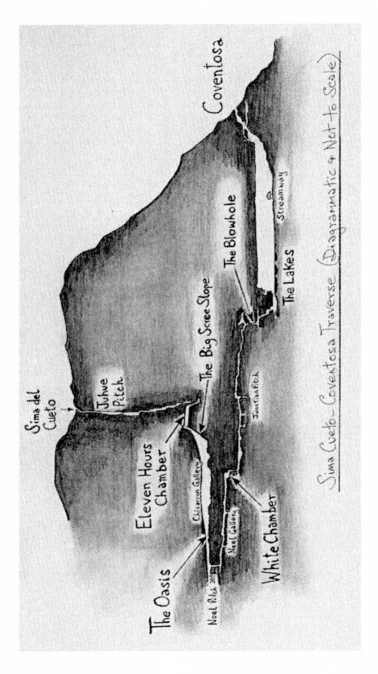

Sima Cueto—Coventosa Traverse

Our docking at Santander took place in a torrential downpour; a usual welcome from the Costa Verde. After some delay, we disembarked in a long queue of cars, passed through the customs and were soon sitting in an excellent fish restaurant near Somo beach. Here we had a superb lunch which included some of the best squid in black gravy imaginable with countless other fish varieties to follow, all washed down with an excellent Rioja. Some hazy time later, we managed to locate the Belgians' campsite that was hidden in a maze of narrow lanes nearby. Here we left a message to let them know we had arrived and would keep the rendezvous on Sunday afternoon. We then drove inland to Matienzo.

As we came over the col that guards the Matienzo valley from the coast, the sun broke through. By the time we arrived at Pablo's bar, the puddles had almost evaporated. Pablo was not there, but his mother told us that an Englishman had arrived on a motorbike and was camping nearby. At the campsite there was only one small tent, pitched quite close to the midden, but no other signs of life. We had the pick of the site. After some thought, we chose a position well away from potential revellers and as far from the parking zone as possible, drawing on previous sleepless experiences from the year before. We soon had our tents pitched and a brew on the stove.

The lone Englishman turned out to be 'Slug,' a caver with considerable experience of the area, who had completed the traverse from Sima Cueto to Coventosa the year before. In the bar that evening, Keith and I explained our plans and persuaded 'Slug' to take us into Coventosa as far as the lakes on a reconnaissance trip. In 'Slug's' opinion, the route finding was generally quite straightforward, except at the Coventosa end, so the reconnaissance would be useful and we could check on the water levels after the recent rainfall.

The next day, Keith, 'Slug' and I drove over to the small village of Arredondo and parked the car at the bottom of the path leading up to the Coventosa porch. 'Slug' reckoned that it would be a dry trip so we took minimal underground clothing in our tackle bags and, as the sun was shining intermittently now, walked up the hill in our shorts and shirtsleeves.

By the time that we reached the entrance we were all quite sweaty from the climb. The cold air emerging from the cave soon chilled us, however, so we changed quickly, lit our lamps and set off into the cave. The entrance passage was high and wide and provided easy going until we came to the first pitch. Here a group of Catalans was fixing a rope for the descent. They were taking a long time to do this but kindly allowed us to attach our rope and overtake them. At the bottom, the route passed through several large galleries, up a couple of rope climbs and eventually led to a traverse high on the left-hand side of a large chamber. The traverse was equipped with a rather ancient, but essential handline into which we clipped ourselves for protection. The descent at the end of the traverse, on a frayed rope, led to a bank of gour pools and eventually down to the main streamway. The torrent swirling along the passage had a full-throated roar to it.

"It was only up to my ankles here last year!" gasped 'Slug' as he plunged chest deep into a 'ford' at one of the numerous crossings. The cave was quite obviously in flood from the heavy rain that had fallen in the last day or two and 'Slug' was amazed to see several new waterfalls crashing down from the roof. The passage to the lakes, normally ankle deep, was filled with a fast flowing river.

We inched our way upstream, clutching the wall to keep our balance on precarious footholds at the waterline, scared that we would fall off and be washed under one of the low slots in the limestone floor where the water disappeared occasionally. After several hundred metres of progress we decided to turn back. At least we would have learnt the most complex part of the Coventosa system. Keith and I decided that, in spite of the extra weight, we would take our wetsuits through from Cueto so that we could cope with the torrent if it was still there in a few days time—a decision that I later regretted.

At the Coventosa entrance, we were surprised to meet some of the Belgians. Francis, Alain, and two others were doing a reconnaissance, too. They aimed to carry in the dinghies, necessary for crossing the lakes, on Sunday afternoon. After a short conversation we confirmed the Sunday rendezvous at their campsite, bid them goodbye and returned to Matienzo.

'Slug' was a most interesting and helpful companion. He had been to Matienzo several times before and knew the area and its caves well. He took us into the Lluega system on the Saturday and, in addition, gave us some clear descriptions of the key moves in the Cueto Coventosa traverse. He would have been a most useful member of our 'English' team, but the bad weather and the sudden arrival of his girlfriend convinced him that he should go climbing in the Picos. He decamped on Sunday morning and we did not see him again until the trip was over.

Sunday morning the mist rose off the valley as the sun arrived and so we decided to spend the day on Noja beach. The day passed quickly as we lazed in the sun, occasionally taking a dip in the sea to cool off, so that it was soon time to visit the Belgians. Although it was not far to Somo beach, the Sunday traffic was quite dense and the journey took longer than expected. In addition, we had difficulty gaining entry to the campsite that was surrounded by high walls and barbed wire. The main gate was guarded by a most diligent fellow who let us in only after we handed over Jenny's passport as a deposit!

We discovered that the Belgians had reserved a separate area on the site to cater for their numbers…forty, including children. On our arrival we were made most welcome. Alphonse and Yvonne, Pierre and Janine and their children were pleased to see us. They introduced us to the others…Young Francis, Old Francis, Alain, Danni, Alex, Benoit, their wives and children, and Françoise…it was difficult to remember all of the names in such a short space of time. The introductions over, Keith and I asked about the final caving arrangements for Tuesday.

"There's been a change of plan!" said Alphonse. "We shall start the traverse early tomorrow morning." "There will be two teams and you and Keith will come with me in the first team which will do the rigging." "The second team is in the cave now and should have all the dinghies on the far side of the lakes by this evening. They will follow us through about two hours later; photographing and derigging intermediate pitches. We'll derig the entrance pitches a few days after the traverse has been completed."

Keith and I were a bit shaken at this. None of our gear was ready! We had thought that we had until Tuesday to prepare! By now it was late afternoon, so we would have to get a move on if we were to be ready by the morning! As politely as possible, we said our farewells and hurried back to Matienzo. Whilst Jenny and Catherine prepared a substantial meal as part of our calorie buildup, Keith and I pottered about 'thinking,' rummaging for food and items of caving gear in the car boots, packing our tackle bags, checking our lamps, assembling the climbing gear and trying to fend off the sort of 'D-day' feelings that a major battle generates. After dinner, we went to the bar, but did not stay as long as usual because we now had a six a.m. reveille. In spite of the sudden unexpected excitement, I slept soundly.

Morning dawned fine and after a substantial breakfast we drove to Arrendondo for the rendezvous. Jenny and Catherine wanted to use the car in our absence, so they came with us to retrieve it. Nine a.m. and no sign of the Belgians! Were we at the right place? Perhaps it was nine o'clock at the top? A few minutes later, several cars roared up led by Pierre's big Range Rover…what a relief! Alphonse hopped out of his car and came over to greet us. "There's been a change of plan!" he announced. "The second team did not exit from Coventosa until after midnight, so we've put the start back until Tuesday morning! Today we've hired a mule to carry the big ropes up to the top entrance. If you want to, you can come up with us, otherwise you can have the day off."

Keith and I felt absolutely deflated, having psyched ourselves up for a major trip. On second thoughts, however, we realised that we could take our heavy tackle bags up to the top entrance today, which would improve our fitness and mean less expenditure of energy before the traverse on the morrow. The girls too decided that they would like a walk up the mountain, so all of us followed the line of cars to a farm further up the valley where the muleteer lived.

It took some time to organise the mule. Mateo, the muleteer, was late out of bed and, when he eventually arrived, the loading of the tackle bags, each crammed full of rope, onto the mule proved quite difficult. The Belgians had an interpreter, Françoise, who managed to explain to Mateo what was wanted. The rest of us stood around in the cool of the morning, idly discussing the scenery and the weather, which was clouding over again. A farm dog lifted his leg and made his mark on my tackle bag, which caused some hilarity. The circling buzzards kept a watchful eye on us. The world seemed poised for a happening. At long last, we set off uphill through a maze of small footpaths used by mules and donkeys to bring milk down from the summer pastures high above. Soon we were all perspiring freely as the ascent was rather steep. I was very glad that I would not have to hump a tackle sack tomorrow!

After about an hour of steep uphill walking we had surmounted the main cliffs, crossed a wide ridge covered in rocky outcrops between small pastures and reached the extensive lapiaz beyond. Here Mateo called a halt as the mule could not negotiate the clints and grykes now confronting us. The mule was tethered to a convenient limestone bollard and the ropes were unloaded from the mule and onto our backs. In single file we picked our way through the rocks, moving carefully as we were now heavily laden. The route was waymarked with red or yellow paint marks but in some places these had been obliterated and the track was difficult to follow. Mateo and Françoise, who had reconnoitred the route the year before, led the way.

During the past year, I had received Spanish lessons at an evening class and so attempted to converse with Mateo directly or through the medium of Françoise who could speak good Spanish and French but little English. The conversation was quite taxing mentally because I had to speak without mixing the languages. However, the attempt increased my Spanish vocabulary considerably. After half an hour of walking and scrambling over the rocky terrain we climbed up a small ravine to a grassy depression high on the ridge overlooking the Ason gorge. The track led along the side of the grassy slope to a small hole, barely visible among the long grass. We had arrived! This was the Sima Cueto entrance.

The heavy tackle bags were grounded unceremoniously as we arrived. Each of us was glad to jettison the weight so that we could either sit down or stretch up. Food was unpacked and served in various ways. Most of us had sandwiches and cold drinks, but Alain had a small stove on which he warmed up some soup. The slope of the grass was quite steep so it was not the most comfortable spot for a picnic as it was difficult to avoid continually slipping downhill. Nevertheless, the relaxation from the long uphill climb was most welcome, as was the pleasure of quenching our thirst in the knowledge that it was downhill all of the way back.

Fed and watered, Keith and I inspected the entrance more closely. It was just over a metre high by a metre wide with a compacted peaty floor and presented a blackness among the green of the grass like a large fox's den. Using the available daylight, we cautiously felt our way in, aware that the big 'thousand foot' shaft was only fifteen metres ahead. The muddy floor sloped down steeply to a slight enlargement where we could stand upright. It looked a good place to park our tackle bags for the night. We exited and returned with the bags and stacked them against the wall.

Alphonse and Francis in the meantime had put on their caving gear and were sorting out a single two hundred and fifty-metre rope. They planned to equip the 'big' pitch to a ledge about two hundred metres down, to save time tomorrow. Alphonse attached a hanger to the bolt-hole driven into the rock near the entrance and then Francis ran a handline through to the pitchhead. I don't think that they approved of the way that Keith and I had disdained such security. Their professionalism was impeccable, all of their tackle was designed to the minimum weight and even their clothing had been selected especially for the trip.

Each move was planned with a precision gained from preliminary research and practice. Alphonse and Francis were a perfect team. They were soon over the lip and out of sight. While Pierre and Alain remained at the entrance to await their return, the rest of us left for the valley.

Catherine and I walked down with Mateo. He was a most amusing fellow, full of anecdotes about the groups that he and his mule had portered for, country tales, folklore and jokes about local characters from the village. The walk down to the col passed quickly as a result and we were sorry to part company with him when he took a different route into the next valley to stable the mule. As we started the final descent, the clouds lifted and the sunlight broke through illuminating the valley below. Until now, preoccupied with heavy loads or conversation, we had not really paid sufficient attention to our surroundings. Now we could appreciate the beauty of the steep limestone cliffs gleaming white against the contrast of the red tiled roofs of the houses in the valley far below. Gorse bushes seemed to come alight and the dark peat accentuated the green of the luscious grass. A large bird, probably an eagle, wheeled below us on a thermal. We could see for miles over rugged hilltops and, looking back, we could see that the clouds had even lifted from the summit near Sima Cueto. As the sun became hotter, we realised how relatively comfortable our ascent had been in the cool of the morning.

Once again we returned to Matienzo, but now that our tackle was already at the top entrance, Keith and I could relax and just take on calories to replenish those we had burnt during the day and add a further stock for tomorrow. We ate well in the bar that night on noodle soup and steak and chips but once again, we limited our drinking and went to bed in good time for another early start in the morning.

Tuesday morning was a repetition of Monday's except that we drove straight to the farm at the bottom of the hill below Cueto. The Belgians were there already and Alphonse came over to see us. "*C'est Dday, John,*" he said. "*Bien sûr!*" I replied. "*Tu es certain qu'il n'y a pas un changement du plan?"* Alphonse laughed, and we went uphill, lightly clad and moving quickly in the cold morning air, carrying water and food for surface use only. The climb to the entrance was faster than that of the previous day and, by noon, we were all at the entrance. A brief snack and Alphonse and Francis once again disappeared underground to continue the rigging past the point that they had reached yesterday. The long grass around the entrance waved in the draught and for a while silence reigned. Keith and I put on our caving clothes, buckled up our climbing harnesses and then crouched down in the grass to keep warm. A cold mist was settling in around us as a bank of low cloud broke over the summit. Alain brewed some coffee on his stove and then warmed up a casserole; the rest of us ate what we had and drank the last of the water carried 'for surface use.' After about half an hour, Leon and the older Francis decided to follow on down and, after checking their gear, they too disappeared into the hole in the grass. Danni and Alain, who had eaten his casserole and polished off a mess tin of soup as well, started to prepare their equipment. When they were ready, they shouted down the hole to the others. A queue had now developed at the pitch head, so Keith and I remained hunched up in the grass trying to keep warm. We decided to eat up the remains of a tin of corned beef. There was no bread left and with only cold water to wash it down, it stuck to our mouths like suet. Not a pleasant meal, but we gulped it down on the principle that it would be easier to carry in our stomachs than in a tin!

After a while a heavy silence became established and we assumed that Alain and Danni must have started their descent. I wanted to start too, to move, to expend some of my pent up excitement. However, Keith was in no hurry: he deemed it more comfortable to wait in the long grass rather than hang suspended from a bolt in the nothingness below. The silence affected him too, though, so we too began the preparations for the descent. Lamps lit, harnesses checked, the last drops of water swallowed, we clipped into the safety line and made our way to the pitchhead, leaving the mist and dewy waving grasses to the buzzards.

Keith approached the lip of the Juhue shaft and shouted to Alain below. A muffled reply floated up. Alain had just cleared the first rebelay at about two hundred feet down. Keith was thus free to descend. With the utmost care, Keith attached his descender to the main rope, settled into his harness, unclipped from the handline and slid out of sight. I moved up to get a better view down the three hundred and two metre deep shaft.

The air in the deep Juhue pit seemed absorbent like cotton wool. Far below I could see tiny lights like sparks falling from an aerial firework. As each of the others passed the rebelays, faint calls of *"Libre!"* could just be heard, almost extinguished in the tomblike atmosphere. Although only about ten metres in diameter, the shaft was imposing but without the scary blackness of a wider cavity. The walls looked smooth and fluted and glittered with small crystals in places. It reminded me of a science fiction film that I had once seen where a lift shaft had been cut through a planet, inside which fantastic machines moved slowly up and down, their lights glowing and the scene humming with power.

"Rope free!" shouted Keith...It was my turn to go. I carefully threaded the rope into the bars of my 'Rack' descender (the two top bars had been recently renewed specially for the occasion), unhooked my 'cowstail' from the belay and settled into my sit harness for a long drop.

The rope hung perfectly, a few feet away from the rockface, allowing an easy ride. I concentrated on maintaining a steady descent, trying not to overheat the 'rack' and to match my speed to the rest of the group. We were all constrained to move in phase by the placements of the intermediate belays rigged by Alphonse and Francis. Since it was impossible to descend on a loaded rope, each caver could not cross a belay point until the next section of rope was free. I could sense the atmosphere of concentration as each one of us moved, purposefully and in unison down the rope; the silence heightening our perceptions. The next bolt loomed out of the darkness below me and simultaneously I heard Keith's call of "Rope free!" A faint call of "*Libre!*" came from Alain far below like an echo.

The riggers had left exactly enough slack in the top section of rope for me to place a foot in the resultant loop. Slowing my descent, I inserted my 'short cowstail' into the belay and continued descending until my weight was taken on the belay. With practised ease, I removed my rack from the top rope and inserted it into the next section of rope, stood on my right foot in the loop of slack to release the 'cowstail' and resettled in my sit harness. I resumed my descent, the atmosphere of depth engulfing me like treacle. I fancied that I could feel the heat radiating from my rack on my cheek. At the next rebelay, the top bars were so hot that I had to flick them out of the upper rope quickly to avoid burning my fingers. I spat on the rack and it hissed, losing some of its heat in the process. Logic told me that the rope would not melt with its poor heat conductance and the meagre heat capacity of the rack, but I was, as yet, only halfway down the rope! One more changeover and I landed on a small ledge. Here there was a puddle in which I quenched the rack to give me peace of mind. This ledge, at minus one hundred and ninety seven metres, was a convenient respite before the final third of the Juhue shaft.

We began to bunch together as the frequency of the rebelays increased. There were at least four rebelays in the next hundred metres of descent. The bottom of the pitch led to a landing with a small window in the rock through which we had to pass to reach the next series of pitches. Rebelay followed rebelay. Occasionally Keith, Alain and I met up at a bottleneck, but the descent was quite rapid as Alphonse and Francis rigged pitch after pitch below us with minimal delay. The pitches became smaller and the walls began to draw in as I entered the lower reaches. Here the rock was wet from a rain of water droplets that seemed to hit the exposed parts of my anatomy with uncanny accuracy. I could hear Keith below me, just past the wettest section, and shouted down to him to find out if I could get through quickly to avoid a wetting. On his affirmative, I slid down the next constricted rift until I was on the section of rope just above Keith. Unfortunately, I landed directly under a small rivulet that was difficult to avoid in the confined space and, as it happened, Keith ran into a problem. I remained under the icy trickle for what seemed like hours, lamenting my fate and complaining to Keith who was struggling below me. Anyone but Keith would have had less patience with me, but he quietly resolved his difficulties and eventually the rope slackened and he called that the rope was free. With immense relief I manoevred into the final length of rope and soon discovered the problem. A knot! The last rope was about thirty feet short of the bottom and Alphonse had tied another rope onto the end of it. Unfortunately he had neglected to leave a loop to clip into. I pulled out an ascender on my safety cord and attached it to the rope. Then, bracing my legs and back against the walls of the shaft, which were close together at this point, I rapidly unclipped my rack from one side of the knot and just as quickly inserted it into the last section of rope. The ascender was released easily and I sank into my sit harness. Not the 'Whernside' way to pass a knot, but quite effective in the circumstances. I dropped down to join the others, all busy removing their harnesses in an enormous passage populated by housesize boulders. The first phase of our traverse was complete.

Alphonse and Francis had been waiting for some time and so were anxious to be on the move. Each carried a compass on his wrist and they determined that we should go due South. Along the vast passage we had to locate 'Eleven hours Chamber,' socalled because the first group to find the way on spent eleven hours looking for it! Alphonse, however, told us what to look for and we all clambered around the massive boulders, looking for a "large letterbox," two metres high by twenty metres wide, at roof level. Somehow or other I happened to be the first to find this after climbing up a steep boulder pile. Beyond lay the large 'Eleven Hours Chamber.'

After a couple of hundred metres of walking through the chamber, we came to the edge of a steep scree slope descending for about two hundred feet and inclined at about forty-five degrees to the horizontal. We decided that the safest thing to do was to descend in a single group. In this way, falling rocks and pebbles would not travel far if they were to hit anyone. Unfortunately Danni, Alain and Leon stopped to take photos, so halfway down the slope the rest of us suddenly came under fire as rocks the size of footballs came hurtling out of the blackness. As I dived for cover screaming, "Stop!" I saw one rock miss Keith's head by a couple of inches. Luckily no one was hurt, and the culprits at the top stopped moving, but it was a very dangerous situation. Large and beautiful as it was, the cave was still a dangerous entity!

At the bottom of the 'Big Scree Slope,' the 'Chicarron Gallery' stretched before us. About thirty metres high and wide the gallery was reminiscent of the large boulder-strewn passages of the Pierre St. Martin. The huge passage continued for over a kilometre of 'hill and dale,' alternative climbs and descents, until we came to a major junction. Here we kept to the left looking for the meagre water supply of the 'Oasis.' The floor became sandy and the passageway became smaller. A few drips were seen on the left-hand wall and in a small alcove in the rockface, a tiny plastic cup had been left to collect the drips for passers-bys, like a roadside shrine. This must be the 'Oasis' surely? Alphonse was certain that it was not, however, and even when we came to an obvious campsite, he still wanted to carry on. He was unanimously overruled, and we all sat down to slake our thirst and eat a meal; as far as we were concerned, this *was* the 'Oasis' and we deserved a rest!

Keith and I unpacked our provisions: peanuts, raisins, pâté, a large tin of steak, a large tin of stew and some 'hard tack' army biscuits given to us by Jack Sheldon many years ago. I emptied the contents from both of the tins into a mess tin extracted from my tackle bag and Keith lit a large solid-fuel stove that he had been carrying. To pass the time while the meal warmed, we munched peanuts and raisins and polished off some orange juice, sipping the liquid through straws inserted in the rectangular paper containers. Each of us carried two litres of water to drink and so far a third had been consumed in the sweaty work through the Chicarron Gallery. The Belgians each had special selfheating tins that they ignited. Soon the rich smell of soup and gravy wafted around the 'Oasis.'

Keith armed himself with a plastic teaspoon. I unpacked a metal dessertspoon and we attacked the hot contents of the mess tin. Although it may sound unfair, the two implements had equal feeding rates. Keith could eat his small portion straight away and whilst I blew on my larger spoonful to cool it down, he could reach in for an extra mouthful for every one of mine! The warm meal was most nourishing and having consumed it, we relaxed against the sandy bank behind us, nibbling chocolate for dessert.

It was now about seven in the evening. Alphonse and Francis had entered the cave just after noon and I had started my descent at about two o'clock, so we had been underground for only five hours—but it was twelve hours since breakfast. I noticed that Alain did not have his stove with him. He had eaten the contents of his 'warm' tin and was ferreting in his bag for other sustenance. I was amazed that he looked so slim with his enormous appetite. One of my water flasks was empty, so I filled it up at the alcove for use in my carbide lamp and then we were off on the march once more.

The dry gallery continued, now much smaller than the immensity at the start of the Chicarron and we soon warmed up again. At one point the passage turned sharply to the right and shortly after that, we came to the top of the 'Noel' Pitch. A tatty rope was in place, leading off a large boulder and across to the far wall where a rusty hanger had been planted. Alphonse rigged the climb with a new rope and descended the twenty-metre pitch, shouting up to confirm that it was the way on.

I was one of the last to descend and when I landed the chamber below was empty. I moved forward and chimneyed down a dry rift into the Noel gallery where large flat slabs of fallen rock paved the floor. The place was very dry and dusty, in marked contrast to the rest of the cave that we had seen so far. Gypsum crystals and encrustations were everywhere and as the passage descended, always steeply, all sorts of beautiful crystalline forms could be seen. The most bizarre forms resembled long strands of cotton wool, hanging from the sidewalls. This was the fabled 'Papa's beard.'

Several climbs over holes in the floor followed and at one of the wider parts a handline had been left in place over a thirty-metre drop. Here I caught up with the others and from then on we moved as a group. The passage went on and on, quite narrow and dry with climbs and descents making progress and route finding very difficult. Alain and I brought up the rear and occasionally we had to shout to ascertain the correct route for fear of losing the way. I remember several hairy climbs over deep black holes, with only small crystals for footholds and friction grips for the palm of the hand. Eventually we all congregated at a steep rope descent. One by one we slid down into the superlatively decorated 'White Chamber' or 'La Salle Blanche.'

La Salle Blanche was truly magnificent! White gypsum encrustations and calcite concretions were everywhere, glittering in the light of our lamps. A stalactite of gypsum hung from the left-hand wall and when we walked into a narrower passageway, the walls were covered in Gypsum flowers, 'Papa's beard' and jagged pillars of crystal. We had to pick our way through, trying not to spoil the formations on which we had to climb. I felt like a gnome in a jewel chest. This must surely be one of the most beautiful and prolific crystalline displays in the world.

Ahead, Alphonse and Francis were having problems finding the route. Alphonse descended a thirty-metre pitch that unfortunately came to a dead end. The rest of us were quite happy to sit down and gaze at the beauty around us and had to be goaded to get up and try to find the correct route. Keith and I returned up the crystal climbs and through the glittering portals to find another passage, studded with gypsum flowers, that continued to a large chamber ending in a deep pitch which had a very old rope down it. I cautiously climbed over to look at the hangers, which seemed robust enough, and pulled up the rope to inspect it. The sheath was badly worn in places and since the pitch was 30-metres deep, we attached Alphonse's second rope, hopefully to be retrieved later by the second team and descended.

The last part of the pitch was a steep slope into a sandy chamber with the 'Speleodrome' gallery driving off to the east. We walked steadily along this gallery until we reached the 'Junction Pitch,' a sudden drop of several metres on a corner. The 'Junction' pitch was already equipped with a ten-millimetre thick rope attached somewhere overhead and out of sight so that we had to rely entirely on an unknown belay. We did not descend this pitch but swung out on the traverse line over the 'Junction pit' itself before ascending the rope for another thirty feet through a narrow constriction to gain a platform overhead. The acrobatics involved were complicated in my case, as I somehow managed to trap my left boot in one of the loops in the handline and so losing valuable energy and equilibrium.

A stream of water drops fell from the roof here and each of us used a mess tin to capture the precious fluid, the watery impacts providing metallic music to shatter the silence. A small tube led off from the platform to a short climb into a rather narrow passage, reminiscent of English caves. This provided fairly easy going for several hundred yards until we came to a complicated area where we had to cross two deep potholes on scanty holds. The route became quite small and tortuous. It was quite tiring to squeeze along the rough tubes and crevices where we had to crawl in places, and where our tackle bags snagged on protrusions from time to time. Luckily Alphonse found the route without much trouble, but Alain and I had to sit it out uncomfortably several times whilst those in front manoeuvred themselves through the various obstacles. Unfortunately for us, as soon as we caught up with them in a comfortable chamber or a handy resting-place, they would immediately take off again! Rifts and small climbs and pitches led us eventually to a series of draughty tubes and then down to the narrow slot of the 'Trou Souffleur' or 'Blowhole.' This was the key link between the Cueto and Coventosa systems.

A fixed rope of some age was already in place for the descent, but the advice was that one should not attach a descender to avoid getting it jammed, as the rift was fairly tight. 'Slug' had said that the airflow was so strong that it seemed like sinking into quicksand. By now it was early morning and the airflow at gale force, but not enough to support my weight at all! Most of my weight was, however, taken by small lumps and knobs on the sides of the rift that descended vertically for about fifty feet. The last part of the rift opened out suddenly and I had to hold on tightly to the rope to prevent myself from falling. Slightly disheveled, my eyes full of grit and my lamp out, I dropped into a sandy chamber where the rest of the team had gathered. My arrival was the signal for them all to get up and move off as the first arrivals were beginning to feel cold!

The passage developed into a steep calcited slope and at one point it was necessary to slide down and be caught by two preceding cavers to avoid slipping to destruction over a small cliff. I don't know how the first two managed it, but I was glad to see that when my turn came that Danni and Keith were the 'catchers.' After this, the passage became larger and led to an extensive boulder pile in another large chamber, 'The Sshaped Chamber.' Here some time was spent searching for a way down to the streamway below. I sat down to restore my carbide lamp whilst all this was happening, and by the time that I had the flame at a suitable brilliance to help in the search the way had been found.

Down between the huge blocks we scrambled to a short climb down a fixed rope and then over a large pool on a traverse line attached to the right-hand wall of the passage. Beyond the traverse was a short beach and then a steep climb up a boulder slope and eventually we came to the innermost of three lakes. Several dinghies, already inflated, were parked at the water's edge ready for embarkation. Sunday's team had done a good job.

It was my impression that the original plan was to have a meal here and I was quite looking forward to that as the weight of my tackle bag was beginning to have its effect on me. However, with the second team hot on our heels, Alphonse was keen to continue straight out and so everyone prepared for the crossing. Keith and I grounded our tackle bags, removed our light overalls and thermal underwear and changed into wetsuits. The Belgians put on their rubber *pontonières* and started to make arrangements for the ferries.

Alain, Danni and Francis had *canards*, or rubber rings with braces on, which allowed them to float waist deep, yet dry in their *pontonières*, so that they could paddle across solo. The rest of us would use small dinghies, although there was a big grey three-man dinghy for the second team to use. Unfortunately Francis' *pontonière* sprang a leak. (In my experience this always seems to happen. Light as they are, *pontonières* are not as robust as wetsuits!) He thus had to take a place in one of the dinghies to avoid exposure, as the lake was 150 metres long and icy cold and followed by another lake 100 metres long and a final lake 50 metres long.

I did not fancy using a *canard* in a wetsuit, nor did Keith, so one of us would have to wait for the next party and travel in the big dinghy. I decided to stay and Alain, who was taking a snack, stayed with me whilst the others paddled off across the lake.

The big lake was about five or six metres wide with the roof rising twenty to thirty metres high above it and the small flotilla of dinghies and canards lit by carbide lamps could be seen for a considerable distance like shrimp boats in the night. We did not have much time to gaze on this eerie yet beautiful scene before the second team arrived. They soon organised themselves and I obtained a place in the big dinghy with Thierry and Alex. Almost an hour behind the others, the second flotilla cast off and, canards following, we too paddled the Stygian waterway to the far shore. An awkward portage, and then the next lake that had several underwater boulders to avoid, was negotiated. A further portage and a short lake and we were in the Coventosa mainstream passage. There was no sign of the first team, so Thierry sent Alain, Gaetan and me on with *canards* and rope in our tackle bags whilst he, Alex, Josef and Toni deflated the dinghies and stowed them for transport on their backs.

The streamway was ankle deep. No signs of the torrent that Keith, 'Slug' and I had seen previously. I had lugged my heavy wetsuit all the way through for nothing! Still, it was a sensible precaution, but by now I was beginning to feel tired because of it. I had been underground now for about eighteen hours and without sleep for about twenty-four, my lamp was on the blink again and I was getting slightly irritated with my tackle bag. Since I knew the way, I led Alain and Gaetan down the streamway and over the various rocks, crossings and junctions to the start of the high level climbs and traverses where the fixed ropes were in place. However, before venturing on the climbs I just had to mend my lamp, without the aid of spectacles and tired and irritable as I was! This took precious time and energy and Thierry and the others overtook me so that by the time that I was ready to move again only Josef and Gaetan, who was also tired, were behind me.

At the exit of the final traverse, high up on the wall, my carbide generator snaplink caught in the handline. Poised over the abyss and obliged to hang on with both hands, I could not free myself and Alain bravely returned to reach around my back and release me. From then on, the way out was straightforward and I found the correct route without any problems. Soon we were at the final rope pitch leading up to the entrance passage and with one last effort that, too, was surmounted. We could smell the entrance now and soon we could see daylight.

On the threshold of the cave, Alain stopped to shake hands—the finale of a superlative underground traverse. We had brought up the rear together and shared an experience and companionship that we would never forget.

In the sunlight, the grasses and ferns at the cave rim glowed green and bright as our dilated pupils adjusted to the daylight. My tired brain became transfixed by the lush organic beauty of the sunlit world. After the cold and stony splendour of the underworld, the clump of ferns seemed like the jewel in the lotus flower.

I looked at my watch: it was a quarter to ten in the morning. Almost twenty hours underground! Alain and I walked down the hill to sit in the sun with the others and whilst we waited for Pierre to come and pick us up, we toasted each other with a celebratory cognac.

22

The Conference

Stalls, displays, competitions, speeches, a bar, the noise and bustle of people moving about, small groups in animated conversation, friendly reunions, the local worthies dispensing their patronage and wisdom, all contribute to the atmosphere of any village fete, or civic function. Such communal gatherings and rituals reveal the identity of the society that supports them. Individual enthusiasm and involvement combine to create an event with a character and existence of its very own.

The annual conference organised by the British Cave Research Association has all of these characteristics. Held over a weekend in the autumn, it provides an ideal opportunity to observe the British caving scene in all of its social and sporting aspects. The participants, like villagers, come in all shapes and sizes and from all walks of life to contribute to a couple of days of interaction that summarise the key events of the past caving year and provide useful material for the future. Behind the scenes is a team of dedicated and able workers on whom the success of the whole venture depends.

Cavers trained to extract money or prepaid tickets from delegates guard the entrance. No amount of friendly chat will gain free entry and it is always important to calculate whether to buy a ticket for the two days or for the Saturday only. The organisers are experienced in fixing the programme of events so that there are always a few things worth seeing on the Sunday, so this requires considerable thought...particularly if one is going to the overnight entertainment provided!

Having surmounted the entrance obstacles and obtained a programme of events, the next thing to do is to sit down and decide what
to see and which lectures to attend. The lectures and competitive
events such as SRT races and tackle bag stuffing run in parallel so, once
again, one has to choose. Alternatively there are the stands manned by
the purveyors of caving gear...temptation to spend on the latest gadge-
try, or else to snap up a bargain!

In addition to the commercial stands and exhibits, some of the
larger caving clubs provide their own stands. These are decorated with
maps and surveys of the club's latest discoveries, with large photographs of recent finds, or artistically framed pictures of underground
formations. The chitchat between rival clubs can be quite amusing to
listen to and is often more enlightening than a boring lecture on cave
mud in Outer Mongolia. The clubs who exhibit certainly advertise
themselves effectively, but how many new members are attracted is not
known...it seems to be more of a social service that they provide.

Around the entrance foyer and in suitable positions among the
stands, the annual photographic competitions are displayed for all to
see. The standard is quite amazing. A few of the competitors are profes-
sional photographers, but most are amateurs although the quality of
their work belies this. To promote cave photography to the caving
population, there is usually a prize for beginners. The photographic
competitions provide an opportunity to see how cavers view their
underground world. Exciting water shots, beautiful formations, glittering crystals, vast pitches and daring moves captured on film, combined
with artistic lighting present the underground scene with a sparkle and
clarity never possible with cavers' cap-lamps. It is easy to forget that the
apparatus used to catch these scenes underground had to be trans-
ported with extreme care through some of the most demanding of
environments imaginable. Each photograph is worth a great deal of
sweat on someone's part, hopefully the photographer's, but very often
that of his longsuffering companions! In recent years the number of
entries in the cave video competition has increased. Video recording

underground used to be only for a few specialists, who achieved public acclaim on TV, but the latest technology now enables less affluent cavers to compete as well.

The conference provides good opportunities for networking. In particular, cavers sometimes organise workshops for those interested in specific caving technologies such as surveying, photography, cave art and underground communication. Cave science symposia are run as separate events, so the lectures at the annual conference are mainly of a sporting nature. Nevertheless, the occasional scientific or semi-scientific lecture is sometimes included if it is of general interest. The majority of the lectures are about caving expeditions, new cave discoveries, new equipment, new techniques, regional news and practical topics likely to interest active cavers. The lecturers, few of whom are professionals, deliver their material using the latest techniques available in modern lecture theatres. The style of the delivery depends on their own personalities, with many lectures presented in a light-hearted and amusing manner. Active cavers have little time for boring lectures! Sometimes videos with or without sound effects are used to attract audiences. The ebb and flow of cavers through the doors of the lecture theatres is governed by the ability of the presenters as much as their material.

Humanity has always needed rituals and customs. In addition to cementing tribal solidarity, rituals provide havens of stability in a rapidly changing and often terrifying world. Between the rites of birth and death, we consciously or unconsciously enact rituals as part of everyday life. When we say "Hello," shake hands and say "Goodbye," we are obeying an ancient ritual. Clapping, dancing, kissing and eating and drinking together are further examples. Although the general population may abandon rituals, new ones always emerge to replace them. For many people, football matches, summer holidays and TV 'soaps' fill the gaps left by religious services, holy days and mummers. A study of rituals provides a useful guide to the culture that develops them and a measure of our age.

Caving provides no exception to the phenomenon of rituals. For some cavers, the rituals are often as important as the caving. Most active cavers, however, are probably unaware that they are engaged in rituals and just enjoy themselves. This is particularly true at the annual conference.

Although the annual caving conference is an important ritual, it is not the only one. The annual club dinners, club meetings, caving politics, 'Stomps' and other gatherings are also key rituals. In the second millennium, when people crave instant gratification and are unwilling to commit themselves to long-term objectives, rituals become even more important as a tribal resource. Minority groups such as cavers rely on them for survival. The continuing success of the annual conference is thus a sign that the caving fraternity is alive and kicking and long may it be so.

23

Stari Hrad

Stari Hrad is the deepest cave in Czechoslovakia. Situated in the 'Low Tatras' near the town of Liptovsky Mikulas, *Stari Hrad* is 424 metres deep, has five kilometres of sporting cave, several large chambers, impressive pitches and a roaring streamway.

In the summer of 1989, the Detva caving club, who control access to the cave, hosted the Crewe Caving and Climbing club for the day and guided a trip to the bottom of *Stari Hrad*. As well as arranging the caving trip, they fed us and took us on a tour of the local places of interest. Our day out with the Detva club was the most memorable day of the fortnight that we spent in Czechoslovakia.

We rose at 5.0.a.m., an early start time for a busy day in the Tatras, above or below ground. Our rendezvous was at 7.0.a.m. in a national park that was several miles away from our hotel in Pribylina. We had to gulp down our breakfast to arrive on time. Tom, from the Brno caving club, our essential contact and expedition guide, chivvied us to make haste. He was, after a week of caving with us in Bohemia, beginning to know our western ways and weaknesses. In a similar manner, unfortunately for him, we had become acclimatised to the loud music on tannoys at dawn and had slept on. A dinner of pork, sauerkraut and dumplings, with lots of excellent pilsner was heavy ballast, too. However, Tom, assisted by three other Brno club cavers, Pavel, Blanca and Ivosh, soon had us packed and ready to go. We made our rendezvous with time to spare, much to Tom's amazement.

At the rendezvous car park, we waited for our guides from the Detva club. We did not have to wait long. A bright red Skoda swished into the car park and drew up alongside. A very large person emerged from the driving seat. Tom shook his hand, had a few words with him, and introduced us to him.

Petr, our guide, had discovered *Stari Hrad* and was obviously well built for such a task. He stood six foot seven on a pair of legs like tree trunks. His ruddy face was split by a large smile of welcome. As we shook hands with him, each of us felt the strength of his grip. I noticed that his arms were about the same thickness as my legs. He was a genial giant of the Tatras! He introduced us to his wife, Helena. Although she looked diminutive beside him, she, too, was well built and extremely fit in appearance. Neither of them could speak English, so it was difficult to talk to them directly, although I had a smattering of Czech and survival Russian that came in useful later. Nevertheless, they were so clearly pleased to see us and so welcoming, that their actions spoke better than words.

Tom and Pavel had an animated conversation with Petr and Helena that we could not understand and then they all drove off in the red Skoda. As the dust settled, we wondered what was happening. It seemed typical of Czechoslovakia in those days, there was always so much confusion and bureaucracy that we never knew what would happen next! Blanca and Ivosh, who could speak English, explained that we needed a permit to drive along the roads in the national park. Apparently Tom had only obtained permission to visit *Stari Hrad* and since it was three miles away and about two thousand feet higher up the mountain, we would need to use the cars to conserve our energies for the cave.

About half an hour later, Tom and the others returned. They had obtained the park access permit with some difficulty from the local authorities. However, it had also been decided that Tom and Pavel were not fit enough to qualify for a trip into *Stari Hrad* although Blanca and Ivosh were! Tom and Pavel pulled on their hiking boots and strode briskly along a nearby path for a day's walk in the mountains. They both seemed extremely fit to me and I wondered exactly what we were in for!

Petr and Helena indicated that we should get into our cars and follow them. Their red Skoda set a good pace uphill along the rough forestry road as if to test our western vehicles to the limit. Mel and Adrian followed in a Ford Fiesta, then Jane, Kevin, Ian and me in a Ford Cortina, with Blanca and Ivosh bringing up the rear in their dilapidated blue Skoda. After a hectic drive, we eventually pulled up in a large clearing.

Hundreds of trees had been blown down in the spring gales and the forestry workers had obviously been hard at work to clear up the resultant mess. We parked our cars along the edge of a deep ditch, hopefully well away from the heavy tractors and forestry equipment and took out our rucksacks. Tom had warned us that the uphill walk was quite arduous and would take at least an hour, so we had packed the minimum of food, light and clothing. With no delay, Petr hoisted a large rucksack to his shoulders and strode purposefully up the hillside.

Helena tried to explain that we need not attempt to keep up with Petr, as he had to go ahead to prepare for us. Not understanding her message, we followed him uphill at a fair speed, leaving Helena, Blanca and Ivosh to trail behind us at a more leisurely pace. The track narrowed as we entered the trees and ran alongside a small stream. Petr paused for a moment to point out a hunter's hide in a large pine tree. We managed to ask him what it was for and discovered that it was for shooting bears. As far as I could understand, they had recently shot a bear that weighed four hundred kilograms. If that was correct, that was a very big bear! None of us fancied meeting such an animal, so we stuck firmly to Petr's heels from then on.

As the track became smaller and steeper, Petr tried to explain that we could rest if we wished and paused long enough for Helena and the others to catch us up. I tried to explain that, in spite of looking hot and purple in the face, we would prefer to keep going *"Pomalu, pomalu,"* until we reached our destination. On we went, the gradient becoming even steeper and the path more slippery as we encountered the bare limestone. Eventually the path zigzagged up a precipitous slope among the trees and on to a substantial ledge that ran beneath a high limestone cliff. Petr indicated that we were nearly there. The walk had taken us just over half an hour so far.

The ledge widened and as we followed it around a right-hand buttress in the cliff, we came to a wooden bunkhouse built into a large cave entrance. The bunkhouse was well constructed and carefully sited to avoid snow and rock falls. The heavy timber and steelwork must have bent many a Detva caving club member's back in the portages up the steep hill behind us.

Petr took a set of Allen keys from his rucksack and started to undo a multiplicity of locks on the bunkhouse door. The locking system had been designed to keep out the most determined burglars. To gain entry without the keys would have required explosives! He opened the door and went inside to start his 'preparations' that Helena had mentioned earlier. We waited politely outside, not wishing to interfere, until he re-emerged carrying a heavy bench for us to sit on. Before we could do so, however, he fetched a sheepskin rug that he draped over the bench like a cushion for us. What hospitality! I sank down into the soft sheepskin with a sigh of pleasure after the sweaty climb.

Petr busied himself opening draws; rummaging in cupboards and performing other chores with a brisk energy that made us feel lazy. We offered to help him, but since only he knew where everything was, this was not possible. I went inside to have a look at the accommodation. The bunkhouse had been equipped with several bunks, a stove, and neatly arranged shelves and cupboards. Water was supplied from a siphon pool in the cave. On the back of the door was a list of the total weights carried up by each Detva caver when the bunkhouse was being built. What a Herculean task they had performed to construct this haven!

Petr took some wood shavings from his bag and stuffed them into the stove. He reached into a cupboard and took out a bottle of methylated spirit, uncorked it and sprinkled it liberally over the shavings. Recorking the bottle, he replaced it in the cupboard and lit the fire by throwing a lighted match into the stove. With a whoosh of flame and a roar in the chimney the fire took hold immediately. Petr added several logs from a stack near the stove and it was not long before we could feel the warmth. The little chimney spouted thick white smoke across the roof of the overhang, the occasional sparks being quenched immediately as they hit the rocky surface. Everything had been well thought out, even to the avoidance of a forest fire.

Petr motioned to us to remove our sweaty shirts and put them to dry on an airer above the stove. Then, with most of the 'preparations' complete, Helena and the others arrived. If we had not followed Petr so closely, we would have had an even greater surprise. Blanca and Ivosh were wide-eyed in amazement at the well-furnished bunkhouse, the warm fire and the welcoming seats. Helena spoke to Petr and laughed, pleased at our appreciation and put a kettle on the stove. She then disappeared under one of the bunks and re-emerged with two electric cap lamps. Even in this remote fortress, she had hidden their valuables as an extra precaution!

Whilst we changed into our caving clothes, Petr and Helena pottered about preparing sandwiches and unpacking various items from their kitbags. When the kettle boiled Helena made lemon tea for us. We gratefully sipped the hot tea, as we gazed out over a superb view across the forest to the distant mountains. The day had started very well indeed.

Time passed quickly and as soon as Petr and Helena had changed into their overalls, the cups and utensils were washed, dried and put away. Our surface clothes, rucksacks and all the easily removable items were placed inside the bunkhouse. Petr locked the door and we then filed one by one along the ledge outside that led to the entrance of *Stari Hrad*.

The name *Stari Hrad* means 'The Old Castle.' As we reached the entrance we realised this was a particularly apt name. The narrow ledge passed through an arch in the limestone reminiscent of a castle portal. We stepped through the portal into a medium sized chamber, open on one side like a belvedere, with a magnificent view of the scenery below. There was a wooden rail to prevent people falling over the edge and a small seat for the older members to sit and admire the panorama. In a recess at the far side of the chamber was the route to the underworld. Petr lit his lamp and started the descent. One by one, we followed him into the cave.

We entered a small, steeply descending passage, about one metre wide and two high. Here it was difficult to move quickly, especially for those of us carrying tackle bags on our backs. Unencumbered, Petr moved very rapidly and we had to hurry to keep up with him. Soon we came to a steep flight of steps, hollowed out in dried mud that ended in a twisting, turning, narrow meander. One or two small drops that followed were equipped with short wooden ladders. The tortuous passage eventually ended at the top of a twenty-metre pitch. Here, we queued to descend.

Most of the Czechoslovakian caves that we had visited so far had been equipped with assorted metal and wooden ladders, so it was no surprise to find that the pitch was already rigged. However, the fixed aid was of a type that we had not encountered before. An alloy and wire ladder was in place, but, instead of hanging freely, it was tensioned to bolts at top and bottom, so that it was held almost rigid. This arrangement made descent very easy and rapid. I thought that it would also be very helpful for the ascent on the way out.

The twenty-metre pitch was in a roomy shaft that was completely dry, so the descent was relatively easy. At the bottom, Petr did not wait and set off again as soon as the first two people had landed beside him. However, since we were a small group, the last person to descend was not left far behind and so we spread out in a convoy along the passages that followed. Three small pitches equipped with wooden and steel fixed ladders led to the bouldery *Slepou* gallery. We crossed this to reach the head of the thirty-five metres deep *Hlavna* shaft. This shaft had three sets of the tensioned ladders, with awkward crossovers between each section. The last and deepest section of tensioned ladder had an additional aid. Metal hoops were attached to the ladder to stop cavers from falling off. The hoops were made of alloy strip about three inches wide, bent into a circle about four feet in diameter and attached to two tensioned cables on the side opposite the ladder to allow climbers to lean against the hoops and rest if necessary. Descending with a tackle bag slung from my harness was not easy. The gaps between the hoops were at four-foot intervals, which was just enough to allow the bag to slip between the hoops and become jammed! Since I was the only one with my tackle bag slung like this, everyone else thought the hoops were a magnificent innovation, in spite of my regular cursing.

The way on from the bottom of the *Hlavna* shaft was through a narrow rift where we had to back and foot down a chimney in rough limestone. Every so often there were places where the rift widened and delicate climbing was necessary to avoid falling, or to prevent dislodging rocks on to those below. A complex route through the rift led to a meander and along to the summit of the deepest pitch in the cave, the *Tristarska*. The *Tristarska* was forty-four metres (130ft.) deep in a wide shaft and was equipped with tensioned ladders fitted with hoops. The first part led over the brink at an angle of about forty-five degrees, giving no sense of the drop below. Then, suddenly, after about fifteen feet, the ladder became vertical. At this point, the abyss, with the twinkling lights far below, reminded me of the view from an aeroplane at night. As I waited my turn, my thoughts of aeroplanes diverted to my memories of the Prague underground. It, too, had been an unexpected technological glory—so glitteringly ultra-modern in an ancient city. The hooped and tensioned ladders seemed similar; unexpected technical wizardry in the natural vastness of Stari *Hrad*.

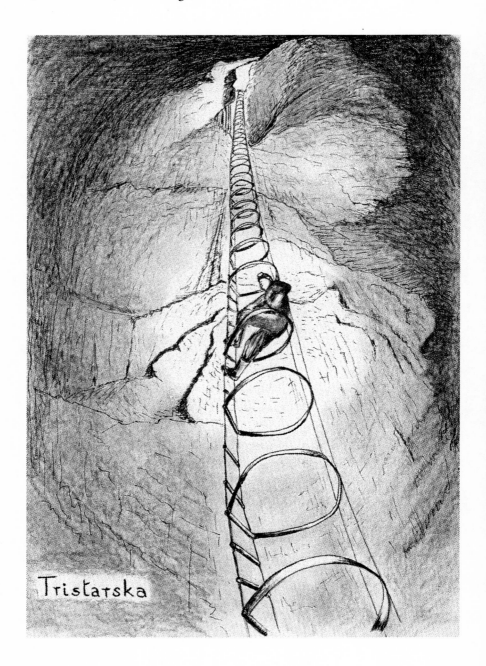

Tristarska

We descended the ladder three at a time, so that the pitch did not act as a serious bottleneck to our progress. The taut cables thrummed like guitar strings under the weight of the climbers. Voices echoed and reverberated eerily in the vast cavity as we called to each other to pass from section to section. Although the depth was significant, all of us made speedy descents. For my own part, I had now devised a way of preventing my tackle bag from snagging, so enjoyed a rapid and exhilarating flight to the bottom.

Helena descended last, and we waited for her at the base of the lofty shaft before following Petr into the huge *'Prieskumnikov Hall.'* Here, our lights could barely pierce the blackness overhead and even the most powerful of our sharp beams only touched the walls faintly. We seemed to be lost in its vastness. Petr led us up a steep slope and along a small path, rather like a mountain track on the side of a valley, to a good viewpoint. He sat down on a large boulder to address us. Blanka translated for him as he recounted that this had been the end of the cave until 1980, when it had ended in a siphon lower down. A team of divers had successfully passed the siphon to discover the extensive passages that lay ahead of us. Subsequently, the Detva club had blasted a way past the siphon to allow normal airbreathers, like us, to gain access to the rest of the cave. The Czechs certainly were not hampered by aesthetic or philosophical caving codes. Petr justified the demolition of the siphon as a scientific necessity. After a brief rest to cool our sweaty selves, we scrambled down a steep boulder pile to reach the erstwhile siphon. The roughly blasted hole was just big enough to stoop through. On the other side, we were able to stand upright in the *'Bielu'* gallery. Here, our massed lamps illuminated a beautiful and colourful landscape that sparkled as we moved to admire the beautiful scenery around us.

On our left, washed by a steady shower of water from above, reared a large boss of reddish coloured flowstone that glowed like a fire in the lamplight. This was *'Etna,'* an aptly named formation in any language. In the cracks and hollows that covered the roof, intricate crystal flowers of Aragonite glittered. We made Petr stop so that we could drink in the view and shine our beams on particular crystals overhead. Adrian took some photographs and then we descended to the *'Buffet pod Etna.'* This seemed to be a sort of cavers' tea-room. On a shelf stood a stove, a kettle, tea-making utensils and saucepans for cooking. All of us were quite hot from the rapid descent 270 metres from the surface, so this seemed a welcome prospect. Petr, however, who was intent on giving us a really sporting trip, kept us on the move. All thoughts of a brew and a rest were shattered.

As we continued our descent, the gallery became larger and eventually opened out into the huge *'Revajov Dom,'* the largest chamber in the cave. The dome-like roof high above was barely visible, even with all of our light beams pointing upwards at the same spot. Petr explained that we were now 300metres below the surface. He then stepped on to the brink of a steeply descending canyon at the far side and disappeared from view. We could see the reflection of his light and hear the noise of his descent, so were able to find the way down with no difficulty.

Several difficult and potentially lethal climbs, sometimes on loose boulders, led down to a huge block jammed in the left-hand wall of the canyon. At this point it was necessary to inch out over a yawning void and reach, at arm's length, to grasp a small piton. Then, taking a firm hold, it was a matter of a dynamic move. A swing out, over the abyss, holding on tightly with one hand, allowed the other to grab a handline that ran behind the block and clip into it. The handline was well secured and in good condition and fixed at intervals in a vertical, relatively tight rift. After all of the safety precautions taken with the previous pitches, it seemed astonishingly dangerous.

The rest of the rift was easier to negotiate as the walls were rough and provided good friction holds for our backs and knees. Ahead, there was a deafening roar of water. No one even tried to shout: we just kept climbing down, our thoughts and senses battered by the noise. Eventually we came to the *'Riecnou'* waterfall. A large stream plunged over the lip and out into space, thundering impressively as it crashed onto the rocks far below. Once again we were amazed at the ingenuity and care that the Czechs had taken to provide a safe descent.

A heavy stainless steel tube had been anchored across the rift. Welded to this, at convenient intervals, were several steel mesh 'Foot-plates.' These enabled us to walk easily above the torrent and reach the top of a ladder pitch without getting wet. The twenty-metre pitch was equipped with a tensioned ladder and restraining hoops. The hoops stopped about half way down to allow climbers to get off the ladder and scramble into an awkward rift that ran along the water channel. Even here, the comfort of the caver had been catered for. A large PVC pipe had been installed to take the main volume of the water. Unfortunately this pipe took up most of the space available and made the descent rather tight and difficult for those of us with tacklebags.

At the bottom of the rift, there was a deep pool across our way. This obstacle was overcome by a sporting traverse around a large boulder with the added spice of a wetting if the manoeuvre failed. Blanca, who was averse to falling in, took some coaxing and masculine help before she gained the other side. Jane, a very competent climber, swung across easily and professionally with no problems.

We were now approaching the bottom of the cave. In the small chamber that followed, Petr showed us a turbine, driven by the force of the water through a series of pipes and valves, that powered an electricity generator. He explained that they were still trying to extend the cave through a tight fissure further on. The electricity was used for drilling shot holes to take explosives. If ever we came again, the cave would certainly be deeper!

After the generator chamber, the rift began to contract until we came to an enlargement where a cross rift intersected a small canal. Here we stopped, as there was just enough room for all of us to sit down comfortably. Petr told us that this was the end of the cave as the canal was impassable. We were now 424 metres below the entrance. Looking at my watch, I calculated that we had taken about two hours to reach the bottom.

Petr and Helena had pocketed sandwiches inside their overalls. I had food for Jane and myself in my tackle-bag and the others had various items of food secreted about their persons. We shared nuts and chocolate and sipped water from a bottle that I had also brought. Petr produced some ripe plums and shared them with us as a most delicious dessert. In spite of the incessant noise of the water and the damp atmosphere, it seemed very cosy in our rocky niche. We talked between mouthfuls of food until our supplies had all been consumed. Petr shook the crumbs from him and prepared for the ascent. The rest of us followed suit, realising that it would be harder climbing out than dropping in.

The ascent went surprisingly quickly, however, apart from the long climb up the *'Tristarka'* where Blanca became very tired. Petr, who had kept back for this eventuality, motored up to her to provide vocal and physical assistance. All of us found that the hoops were of a considerable help. Apart from allowing us to rest and recover energy, they allowed the faster climbers a safe place to wait for the slower ones. From then on we maintained a more sedate pace and steadily made our way upward. In seemingly no time at all we were struggling in the confines of the narrow entrance passages. We soon emerged onto the ledge of Stari *Hrad*, steaming from our exertions and blinking like owls in the bright sunshine. The trip had only taken four and half-hours.

Petr went ahead to unlock the bunkhouse. The rest of us extinguished our lamps, and stopped to admire the view. When we eventually caught up with him, he had already undone all of the locks and was opening the door. He perked up the fire and put some water on to warm. Helena, Jane, and Blanca took off their overalls and disappeared inside for a wash. Petr led Kevin, Ivosh and Ian down the hill to an outside shower that was fed from the sump in the cave behind the bunkhouse. Since the water was icy cold, Mel, Ian and I, who were relatively clean, decided to forgo this pleasure. We returned to the bunkhouse and washed in a bowl of warm water to cries of "Chickens!" It was not long before all of us were re-attired in our surface clothes that had been drying in the hut. We sat admiring the view, wondering what was going to happen next.

Helena, who had been very busy in the kitchen, emerged with some soup, bread and a salad. What excellent hospitality! She and Petr must have carried the ingredients up the hill especially for our benefit. We were most grateful and tucked into a most pleasant and welcome meal, washed down with lemon tea. With the meal, the superb view at our feet, the comfort of the fleece-covered benches and the warm sensation flowing in our muscles from the exercise, it was a truly blissful moment.

Through Blanca, acting as interpreter, Helena explained that we would now take a short tourist excursion to visit some gypsies who lived in a nearby valley. Petr wanted to buy some goat cheese and thought that we might like to do the same. We all helped to wash up the dishes and to tidy the hut. Then, our rucksacks packed, Petr locked the bunkhouse up securely and we started down the steep trail to the valley below. I stood for a while, taking a long last look at the idyllic chalet nestling under its cliff and wondered if any of us would ever return in the future.

The route that we took down was shorter, but considerably steeper than that we had taken for the ascent. In some places, the slippery rocks and grass were quite treacherous. We seemed to arrive at the cars in no time at all. After a pause for photographs, we re-embarked in the cars and drove off, with Petr and Helena leading the convoy. Our route was along forest tracks for about two miles and eventually led to an open field where the gypsies had their camp. Their covered wagons were surrounded by a large flock of goats. Nearby was a huge woodpile, next to which was a rickety old barn with wood-smoke belching from a hole in the roof. Petr shouted something in Czech dialect. A filthy, ancient, gypsy emerged, trailing clouds of smoke around and behind him. This was obviously the cheese-maker! He had a lengthy discussion with Petr and then they both disappeared inside the barn. They came out; each bearing carved wooden mugs brimming with curdled goat milk. The mugs looked decidedly unhygienic, as did the white, lumpy liquid. We were expected to drink it! Not wishing to appear ungrateful, Jane threw caution to the winds and tasted some tentatively. "It's not bad," she said, "It tastes rather like yoghourt." To prove the point, she then swallowed several mouthfuls of it! We all knew that Jane had a stomach like a car-crusher and could eat and drink anything, so none of us felt particularly impressed. Nevertheless, we had to be as diplomatic as possible and there were three mugs to be emptied. I tasted some, too. It was not at all bad, provided that one did not look at the mug too closely. I drank half a mugful with well-simulated relish and this persuaded Adrian and Kevin to take some too. Mel and Ian, always cautious as far as a dose of the squits was concerned, decided that discretion was the better part of valour. Helena, Blanca and Ivosh had no such worries and polished off the remainder, whilst Petr started negotiations to buy some goat cheese.

We had already tasted Czech goat cheese from one of the village markets and in my opinion, it was quite delicious. However, there was a problem. The gypsy only had two cheeses, each weighing about two kilograms and resembling large grimy footballs. This was too much for us to cope with, and the gypsy was unwilling to cut them up. Petr decide to buy one. He argued that he could sell it off piecemeal at his office. The gypsy seemed well satisfied. He wiped his cheesy hands on his milk-stiffened trousers and grinned toothlessly as he took Petr's money. Business completed, we said our goodbyes and returned to our cars for the next phase of the tourist trip that was described rather vaguely as 'A sort of sauna.'

Petr drove down the valley and into the outskirts of a small village. Crowds of people were ambling about in a holiday mood, chatting in groups and idly taking the sunshine. The roadside was littered with badly parked cars and other vehicles. We managed to find parking spaces after several difficult manoeuvres, however. As soon as we emerged from our cars, we could not help noticing the awful smell. The pong was definitely sulphurous and strong enough to make us cough. I wondered if the smell was an after-effect of the goat's milk, but the fart-like stench was actually a local phenomenon. We were approaching a line of sulphurous hot springs that were rising in open country to one side of the road.

Petr explained that the springs were volcanic in origin, and apart from the stink, were supposed to have healing powers. It was for this reason that the crowds had come to the village. There were several places where the springs had formed deep pools and people were bathing. There was also a sort of Buxton Spa building where the water had been piped for drinking. I suddenly realised that this was where we were going to have our 'sauna'! We stripped off our outer garments down to our pants and, choosing a pool with the least sulphur crust at the edge, lowered ourselves in up to our chins. Apart from Ian, who had a hole in his pants, we all enjoyed a communal and therapeutic bath.

The water seemed surprisingly cool at first and felt rather soapy. Sulphurous bubbles, erupting from below, kept the water moving around us. Once we had acclimatised, however, the warmth became more apparent. The sensation of warmth was very relaxing and enjoyable. We sat in a circle, chin deep, intermixed with two hefty middle-aged women who had been soaking there before we arrived. Adrian was rather disconcerted to discover that he was playing footsie with one of these instead of Blanca. He very nearly became the object of desire of a female forklift truck driver! Luckily for him, by the time that things were becoming serious, we decided that we were now clean enough and left the pool to get dressed. The locals must have thought that we were an uninhibited gang as we capered over the grass in our soggy, semi-transparent underwear.

By the time that we were all decently clothed again, the evening was closing in and appetites were sharpening. None of us wanted to return to the unvarying pork, dumplings and sauerkraut at our 'hotel.' We asked Blanca to translate that we wanted to treat Petr and Helena to the best possible dinner locally as a sign of our appreciation for their hospitality. They were able to recommend a restaurant about twelve miles away that had a trout stream alongside. It was agreed unanimously that this would be ideal and we drove there straight away.

We arrived in the gathering dusk, just as the lights were being lit, to be met at the door by the patron. He was an old friend of Petr's and welcomed us in with open arms. A few excellent beers later, in a rosy atmosphere, we ate the best meal of the holiday. Freshly caught trout, crisply fried potatoes and a salad seemed fit for a king after our stodgy fare at the 'hotel.' We managed to converse after a fashion with Petr and Helena as the alcohol loosened our tongues. Petr showed us several books and pamphlets of *Stari Hrad* and other local caves. The evening passed too quickly in such convivial activities. Eventually the celebrations had to end as Petr and Helena had a long drive home to Detva and their bed. They also had to work the next day, so needed a decent sleep. We said our goodbyes in the darkness and watched the red lights of their car disappear into the night. They were two remarkable people, who had given us an unforgettable experience and would remain in our memories forever. All of us hoped that we would meet them again sometime.

24

Notts Two

For dedication, patience, persuasion, skill and sheer hard work, there are no better exponents in the caving world than the cave diggers. These hardy individuals who work above and below ground are the unsung benefactors of the rest of the caving community. The ability to find a promising lead from the geological clues, radio-location, magnetometry, water divining, draughts or other methods has to be augmented by a considerable expenditure of physical, mental and often monetary resources before a discovery is made. The rewards are rare and for every dig that succeeds, there are countless digs that collapse or peter out after years of exhausting toil. The use of explosives, sometimes essential, can be a considerable hazard and hindrance to diggers although in recent years the use of Hilti caps that do not emit toxic fumes has been very successful. Diggers have to be good at civil engineering to shore up unstable digs, too. The disposal of spoil in confined quarters and on the surface without damaging the environment also poses considerable problems to diggers.

Over the years many major cave systems have been discovered due to the efforts of the diggers, often unsung after the initial excitement. Examples of such systems that spring to mind are Ogof Ffynnon Ddu, Daren Cilau and Ogof Draenen in South Wales and Kingsdale Master Cave, Illusion and the Iron Kiln dig to Notts Two in Yorkshire to mention but a few. Ogof Draenen was dug regularly on Thursday evenings for a period of two years before the breakthrough was made. Iron Kiln was dug for over twelve years before reaching Notts Two and the deep entrance shaft is a monument to the skill and endurance of the diggers.

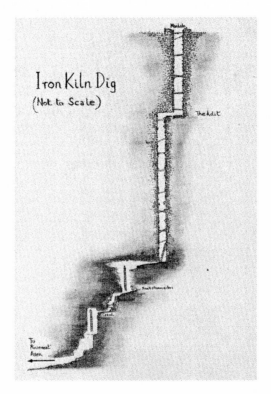

The history of the Iron Kiln dig is most interesting. Colin found the dig site when he stopped for a smoke whilst cycling across Leck Fell. He was sitting on the ground in a small depression among some old iron workings just off the road. Comfortably set, he lit his cigarette, inhaled and shook the match to extinguish it. As he did so, he noticed that a draught coming from beneath him blew the smoke from the dying match-head. Puffing on his cigarette, he bent down and removed the heather and earth around the source of the draught. The draught strengthened, blowing his cigarette smoke into his face. The boulder ruckle that he had uncovered connected to a source of air below! Realising the potential, he hastened back to Ingleton to fetch help and the dig was started with considerable enthusiasm. However, Leck Fell did not give up its secrets that easily and a year later, the dig was still going downwards into a mass of stones and boulders, probably used by the ironworkers to fill a large hole in the ground. The lack of a solid rock face meant that the dig had to be stabilised to prevent its collapse. Nevertheless, Colin persevered with it, encouraged by the draught and sustained by the patience of Job.

Over the years, Colin's dig, soon to be named Iron Kiln, attracted many helpers, some of whom came and went with the draught, as the dig became deeper and deeper. The lack of a rock face became more of a problem as the dig became deeper. To prevent the dig entombing the diggers, scaffold poles, wooden beams and cement were installed to shore up the walls of the dig all of the way down to the digging face. Spoil removal soon became a significant problem. Not only was it hard work to haul the debris up an increasingly deep shaft, but the piles of stones and broken rock on the moor soon began to attract attention. The work of 'landscaping' the spoil heaps to hide them was an extra burden. As a consequence, the final breakthrough into Notts Two did not occur until over twelve years later. The success was rapidly transmitted around the local caving community and soon reported in the caving press with exciting photographs. It was the first great caving breakthrough of the new millennium!

Once the caving grapevine hears of a successful dig, all of those 'in the know' try to visit it as soon as possible. The thrill of exploring the finds before they are gated or spoiled by hordes of visitors is spiced by the potential for new discoveries. In the case of Ogof Draenen, I was lucky enough to be taken on a visit fairly soon after its discovery. In the case of Notts Two, however, it seemed as if the fates conspired to keep me out. Firstly, I had lulled myself into believing that the dig would never 'go' and so did not react quickly when Colin told me that it had 'gone.' Secondly, I had never studied the reports of the exploration of Notts Two by the divers in the late eighties and was unaware of the extent and beauty of the system. Thirdly, the Foot & Mouth outbreak closed Leck Fell and the surrounding areas for nine long months. Fourthly, when access to the fells was allowed I was overseas. Hence, it was not until early in 2002 that I could arrange a visit. Unluckily, the week before my trip was one of the wettest of the winter. The final straw was that on the day planned for the descent it poured in torrents and the trip had to be abandoned. However, determined to see the wonders of Notts Two, we sat the weather out for a few days until the rain eased and it was safe to descend. It was well worth the patience although nothing like that of the diggers!

It was thus that, one Sunday morning after twenty-four hours without rain, Keith drove me up to Leck Fell to descend Iron Kiln and visit Notts Two. The entrance was in a hollow near the road and surrounded by several landscaped spoil heaps. A few scaffolding poles were lying on the ground nearby. The entrance itself was a raised manhole in concrete with a rectangular iron plate as a lid. Keith removed the lid and there was just enough room for him to squeeze through to a wooden platform above a deep scaffolded shaft. A couple of buckets made from plastic bins, piles of old rope and other bric-a-brac were scattered on the platform. Several old ropes and a pulley system hung down the shaft. An aluminium ladder, attached to the platform, gave an easy descent for the first few feet. Keith climbed down on to the scaffold poles so that I could get in and close the lid. I had brought a bag of rope and some climbing gear with me, so found this to be a struggle. Once I was safely on the platform, I looked down the shaft. Keith had begun to climb down and had made rapid progress. I could see his light about thirty feet below me in a tangle of poles and struts around and across the shaft. I decided to leave my tackle bag on the platform as the shaft was quite constricted and had lots of hand and footholds that made a roped descent unnecessary. I gingerly climbed down, trying not to catch my cell or my climbing harness on the countless bolts and other projections that littered the shaft. As there were plenty of hand and footholds, I was spoilt for choice. The main problem was to choose which way to pass the occasional crossed poles that braced the dig at regular intervals. The last section of the entrance shaft was walled with breezeblocks on one side, so I could insert my feet for regular footholds and slide down with my back to the opposite wall. At the bottom, there was a short tangle of poles and a loose plank of wood on the floor. I could see Keith's light reflecting through *'The Adit'*—a short rocky connection to the top of another shaft. I crawled through, noticing a bucket still on its pulley at the shaft top and stood on a shiny scaffold pole to have a look at the next section. The second shaft was deeper than the first, probably eighty feet deep as far as I could estimate. I stepped down onto the next scaffold pole, turning to avoid a protruding clamp, and then continued climbing down. I soon established a rhythm in my descent, even though the poles were not regularly spaced. At the bottom there was another aluminium ladder for a rapid descent of the last few feet. I could not see Keith's light, as there was a low crawl at the bottom. I lowered myself into it and wriggled forward to emerge in a small rift. Keith shouted to me from the other side, advising me to traverse across the top. I joined him at the top of a short pitch in the rift where there was an old 'Electron' ladder to aid our descent. At the bottom was a short section of passage containing a small stream. A section of aluminium ladder led down to a small chamber, followed by a constriction that had scaffold poles holding the rocks at bay. Here there was a shower of water, barely diverted by an old blue tarpaulin. Not wishing to get soaked, I wriggled through as quickly as I could into a flat out low crawl. Luckily the crawl was quite short and emerged into a larger section of rift passage, again equipped with an 'Electron' ladder for descent. Here I found that the rift was quite tight. I could not insert my feet easily into the rungs of the ladder, so went down it hand over hand. A short passage followed until it was necessary to climb down an awkward rifty corner to gain the floor of a larger passage. A small stream ran along the floor and soon we came to a chamber under a high aven with ropes hanging down it. We had reached 'Mincemeat Aven' and were now in inlet thirteen of Notts Two. Until the breakthrough from Iron Kiln, this had only been accessible by cave divers.

The descent had made me sweaty and overheated in my heavy PVC oversuit, so I gladly followed Keith along an easy passage into a small chamber where we paused for breath. Keith pointed out a muddy crawl that was a short cut to the upper streamway, but as this was my first visit, we continued down to the Notts Two streamway a short distance further on.

The stream was running in full spate from the recent heavy rains, its current accelerated fiercely in a narrow trench. The trench had been incised over the years into the floor of a larger passage by vadose action of the stream and we could see the roof high above. The noise was tremendous as the humming sound of the flooded streamway echoed around the cave. Where the water ran smoothly in the trench it had the clear brown beer colour of peat stain. Where it cascaded over boulders and swirled around corners, the turbulence, froth and spume made it sparkle whitely. We pushed on upstream, fighting the force of the knee-deep water.

We passed several inlets as we continued upstream with the roof high above us. I remember that one, probably 'Sir Digby Spode's inlet,' entered where the passage was very large and high, with a rope hanging down temptingly from above. Shortly after this point we stopped to admire a magnificent calcite column connected to a large flowstone boss on the wall above us. The whiteness of the formation was accentuated against the blackness of the void above. This was just a taster for things to come!

Although Keith mentioned it, I cannot remember exactly when we passed 'The Nick Point,' but suddenly the character of the passage changed from a high angular (vadose) cross-section to a more rounded (phreatic) cross-section. The trench disappeared and the water ran more smoothly and was sometimes deep in places where the passage narrowed. One significant change was that we saw more beautiful calcite formations. There were transparent helictites and flowstones on the walls together with a few black stalagmites and flowstones. Such formations are quite rare, the black colour deriving from manganese salts. There were also groups of rippling shiny curtains—some of them striped with black like tea-towels. It was an incredibly beautiful sight after the dull days of winter outside.

We soon came to a sandy inlet on the right. Here we climbed out of the water and up a sandbank to look at a small excavated crawl at the top. From the summit of the sandbank I could see a humped mass of black flowstone protruding from the sandy slope down. It had five or six white circles of stalagmites dotted along it like a negative of a ladybird's back. What a remarkable place this was! Keith's curiosity and my visual hunger were soon satisfied, so we climbed back down to the streamway and continued upstream passing yet another inlet on our left.

Overhead were sparkling white stalactites of all shapes. Long pointed stalactites and straws hung in the roof together. Here, the roof was about forty feet high, but soon we passed under a higher dome and made good progress until we came to a section of deep water. Although we tried to choose the shallowest routes wherever possible, at one place, a chest-deep wade in the icy water was unavoidable. Luckily this section was quite short and it was a pleasure to gain the shallows on the other side and warm ourselves up. Further upstream we passed under 'Vlad the Impaler'—a large pointed stalactite with a curtain shaped like a wing at the top. Shortly after this point we reached Curry Inlet on our left. Here we took a scenic detour.

Curry Inlet was an immediate surprise, even after the formations in the main passage. On one side, beautiful curtains were arrayed for several yards. Pristine in appearance, they shone sparkling white in alcoves and on the walls, curving and flowing like a display of drapery in a wedding shop. On the other side, easily overlooked due to the beauty of the curtains, were helictites. Some helictites, shaped like transparent fingers, beckoned on ledges. Others curled white and complex like frosted twigs or stag's antlers. Further along the passage, past the curtains, straw stalactites hung from the roof like misty clouds against the black background. In places where the roof lowered, taped pathways prevented us from damaging the straws overhead. Although the calcite formations were well protected by the tapes, I noticed that the mud formations were left to take their chance. Apart from the dendritic mud patterns there were several lovely mud stalagmites shaped like little wooden egg-cups that deserved preservation. With their lack of colour and camouflaged on the floor or walls they are easily trodden down.

Trying to see as much as we could, we went slowly to the end of Curry Inlet to where there was a silt choke and a large sandbank. To one side, the passage continued low and watery, but it looked fairly well decorated. Keith told me that it led to a crawl and a final sump. It seemed to me that it was best left for another day, so we decided to retrace our steps back to the main streamway. Although it was only about three hundred yards away, we took our time, frequently stopping to take in new views and formations that we had missed on the way in. Eventually we arrived back at the junction, where the stream seemed noisier than when we had last heard it.

"Fancy a look upstream?" Keith asked laconically. "It's waist deep in places and ends in a swim." Upstream, the passage looked rather gloomy to me after the dazzling beauty of Curry Inlet and, for a moment, I wondered whether the journey would be worth it. However, since I had never seen what was there, I decided to just have a look, so led the way upstream. It was a wise decision!

The upstream passage provided really enjoyable caving. The roof was just the right height to show off the occasional decorations and straws hanging from the ceiling. The passage was comfortably wide enough to make the going easy and the whole aspect was of a place new and untouched by humanity. It was a magnificent stream passage by any standards and I would have been stupid not to take such a marvellous opportunity to see more of it.

We paddled, boulder hopped and waded upstream, passing two deep cold pools that were more than waist deep. Keith pointed out Inlet Five, suggesting that it was worth a visit in the future and soon we came to a large passage on the right that was blowing out spray and wind. This was *'Daylight Aven'* and around the corner there were several routes into *'Paschendaele'* off to the left, before the water deepened to swimming depth. We climbed out onto the rocks to dry out. From our vantage point we looked as far around the corner as we could. Ahead it looked very deep, so we decided to turn back. On the corner behind us, where there was an eddy with a cake of froth rotating in its vortex, I had noticed that there was froth on the wall about six inches above the water level. Even though the water levels were falling, we did not know what was happening on the surface. With more rain forecast, it seemed a good idea to leave whilst the going was good.

We made a fairly rapid return downstream, stopping only briefly to look at favourite formations, our feet and legs beginning to feel the chill of constant immersion in cold water. After the *'Nick Point'* the current in the narrow trench was now behind our knees, so we had to make sure to place our feet firmly to avoid having our feet washed from underneath us. This was particularly important on the small cascades and sharp bends of the passage. Soon we were back at Inlet Thirteen again.

After a brief discussion, we agreed that I should explore downstream as far as the current would allow. I did not know if I would ever have this opportunity again, so did not want to miss out. The downstream passage was quite steep in places and the small cascades and bends contained more volume than upstream, so the going was quite exciting. We were constantly aware of the humming of the flood, a noise that in more dangerous streamways can be quite frightening. I was somewhat disconcerted to see that, further downstream, the cave walls were covered in black with mud as far up as I could see in the beam of my light. It was obvious that in some circumstances, this section could flood to a serious depth! The chance of something blocking the downstream sump seemed remote, however, so I pressed on. We hastened down-stream, passing Gour Inlet on the left and then Tape Inlet on the right. As the trench we were in became larger and the current fiercer, we seemed to be driven along until we came to a series of cascades. There was a tremendous roar of water and driven spray floated in the passage ahead. I climbed up the wall to assess their volume. The next cascade looked passable by bridging across the walls, but the volume of water running over it was so great that if I were to slip in, I would be washed away immediately. Knowing that there was a short drop and a chute beyond the cascades, I felt that 'Discretion was the better part of Valour.' Keith agreed, commenting that it would be harder work returning upstream against the current. I climbed down and he led the way back to Inlet Thirteen at a steady pace. I could only just keep up with him. My lack of fitness and creaky knees were beginning to slow me down!

It was quite a relief to reach Inlet Thirteen. There was a small chockstone guarding the entrance. Keith dipped under it and squeezed up the other side. Foolishly, I climbed over it, wasting a considerable amount of energy in the process. The quiet passage was a pleasant change after the roar of the streamway and we made good progress until we arrived back at Mincemeat Aven. There was then an awkward climb across a corner and into the rift with the 'Electron' ladder. I had easily come down this ladder hand over hand, but to climb up I had to insert my wellie-clad feet into the rungs. The first foot went in easily, but I had to twist and wriggle strenuously to get my other foot on the next rung. The rift seemed to be only the width of my foot! Luckily I only had to climb a few feet before I could get off the ladder into the rift passage above, but it involved another expenditure of my diminish-ing reserves of energy. I could see Keith's light reflecting around a tightish crawl to the left. I followed him, glad that he knew the way, as it was not obvious. The crawl ended in the wet zone held together by scaffold poles, so I forged ahead, trying to keep as dry as possible, to the small chamber containing an aluminium ladder. I climbed this and caught up with Keith who was halfway up the ladder on the next pitch. His carbide light had gone out and he was trying to relight it. As I waited at the bottom, I noticed that the last rung of the ladder was broken. Once he was free, I climbed up and followed him across the rift at the top and into the final crawls that led to the bottom of the second shaft of Iron Kiln. With all the bodily movements, wriggling and crawling, my climbing harness and lamp belt were hanging low on my hips. I took some time in the confined space available to readjust these to make the next ascent more comfortable. From then on it was straightforward, if strenuous, work to climb up the shaft. I frequently had to pause and look upwards in order to choose the best way through scaffold poles. However, I was soon through 'The Adit' and climbing the ladder at the bottom of the top shaft. From there to the surface, it was just a matter of time and energy as there were plenty of holds and I was soon on the platform at the top, puffing and panting with the unaccustomed exertion. In a few minutes I had ascended the results of twelve years' hard work by the diggers!

I switched off my lamp, passed my tackle sack up to Keith who was waiting on the surface, then squeezed up through the manhole and onto the moor. It had been a most enjoyable and memorable trip and I thanked Keith for arranging it for me. Although I could feel one or two muscles aching, I seemed to have escaped with no bruises. I looked around me in the daylight. The weather was still rather overcast and windy, but there were no signs of rain during our expedition underground. Keith replaced the lid and we walked back across the moor to the car, admiring the view across to Morecambe and Heysham under the cloud strata. We changed into our surface clothes, hurrying to keep warm as the wind blew around us and were soon driving down the road to welcoming firesides in the plains below.

How time flies! A month ago, Keith, Colin and I had planned this trip in the bar of 'The Wheatsheaf' and now it was over. The memory of it fresh in my mind, I recalled the sights, sounds and events in my imagination. I tried to store it in my mind along with the vivid memories of other trips made during forty-four years of caving. If only we could control the passage of time! Why does time spent enjoying oneself pass more quickly than that at other times? Time contracts with fun as well as with velocity. Perhaps Einstein missed something? He never went caving, for sure. Anyway, most cavers would choose to lead "A short life and a happy one" although this adage wears a bit thin when they start to draw their state pension.

That evening, as I ruminated by the fire sipping a glass of wine, I decided that there was nothing like a good caving trip to keep one young and happy! Despite stiff joints and wasting muscles, the older caver can always find caves for inspiration and enjoyment. We have to make the best of things whilst the moving finger writes whether we are at the start of our careers or at the end. Although I was now in my 'Third Age,' my caving career was not yet ended!

About the Author

John Gillett was born in Buckingham in 1937 and started caving in 1958 during his National service. He continued caving at university and became president of the university caving club before graduating as a chemical engineer. He then worked in the plastics and pharmaceutical industries for thirty-seven years as a technical manager. During his industrial career he designed, developed and ran several new processes, published many chemical engineering papers and wrote a book on risk assessment. He received an Honorary Doctorate from L'Institut National Polytechnique de Toulouse for his work in the field of chemical engineering education. He retired in 1999 and is now a freelance writer and lecturer.

John is still an active caver and has belonged to several caving clubs in the United Kingdom during his caving career. He is a fluent French speaker who regularly caves with French and Belgian caving clubs. He also speaks Spanish, survival German and a smattering of several other languages necessary in the European limestone regions. He led a successful expedition to the Gouffre Berger in 1983.

He is married with one daughter who is a chartered chemical engineer and caver. He lives in Gawsworth, Cheshire.

Glossary of Terms

Arne Saknussemm: A fictional alchemist in a novel by Jules Verne, who discovered the way to the centre of the earth.

Ascender: A device for ascending a single rope, usually working on the principle of a cam which jams in the rope in a manner such that, whilst the ascender can be pushed up the rope freely, it cannot be pulled down. Using two ascenders, one for the chest, and one for the legs, it is possible to ascend by moving the ascenders one at a time.

Aven: An overhead shaft above a cave passage, usually leading to an upper series.

Bedding Plane: An enlarged lateral joint between two beds of limestone, or in a shale band. Usually wide and low.

Belay: A rock pillar, stalagmite boss, boulder, or hole in the rock to which a ladder or rope can be attached. The use of self-drilling bolt attachments also provide artificial belays for the same purpose.

Breccia: A geological term for broken rock and angular stones cemented together by calcite or lime.

Calcite: A crystalline deposit of Calcium Carbonate.

Canard: A circular rubber ring, inflated for buoyancy and worn with a simple harness to enable the caver to float in deep water.

Carabiner: A metal snap link for connecting ropes or climbing devices to the caver or to a belay.

Carbide: Calcium Carbide. When reacted with water, calcium carbide generates acetylene gas that can be burnt at a special jet to give a bright light. Acetylene: air mixtures are explosive and anaesthetic.

Cave Rescue: Cave rescue is provided underground by teams from local caving clubs. The surface callout and ambulance arrangements are organised via the local police force.

Cowstail: A length of rope or tape used to protect the caver when performing manoeuvres such as passing a belay or traversing a handline. The caver usually has two cowstails, a short one for attaching to a belay when descending and a long one for traverses or for passing a belay when ascending.

Descender: A device for descending a rope. The device acts as a brake and generates heat, becoming hot on a long descent.

Duck: A cave passage almost filled with water, but with just enough air space to breathe.

Existentialist: A person who holds an antiintellectualism philosophy of life, holding that man is free and responsible, based on the assumption that reality as existence can only be lived but can never be the object of thought.

Flowstone: A continuous sheet of calcite on a wall or floor formed by deposition from slowly flowing water.

Gour: A formation around the rim of a pool or basin deposited by water overflowing the rim. The pool deepens as the gour, or rimstone, builds up and forms a 'Gour Pool.'

Helictite: An eccentric stalactite or stalagmite that has elements growing out at right angles to the axis or branches that are usually curved and twisted.

Maillon: The short name for a Maillon Rapide, which is a metal link that has a hexagonal nut which can be unscrewed to attach to ropes or climbing equipment, in a similar fashion to a carabiner.

Merguez: A very spicy sausage, based on recipes of Algerian origin.

Moonmilk: A soft and friable form of calcite sometimes found on the floor of cave passages.

Nirvana: The ultimate objective of Buddhists, that is, to become one with the universe. Enlightenment.

Pitch: A vertical section of cave, normally passed by using a ladder or a rope.

Poignée: A handled ascender for climbing up a rope.

Pontonière: Thin rubber waders worn under a boiler suit. The Pontonière reaches up to the top of the chest and is supported by braces running over the shoulders. The top of the Pontonière can be inflated so that the caver can float upright in water.

Rack: A type of descender which has several alloy bars through which the rope is threaded to provide controlled braking during a descent.

Rebelay: An artificial belay placed at some point along a rope to avoid abrasion or water. A rebelay has to be passed when descending by removing the descender from the section of rope above the rebelay and reinserting the descender into the section of rope below the rebelay. During this manoeuvre, the caver attaches himself to the rebelay by a short piece of rope or tape termed a 'Cowstail.' The reverse procedure is followed for the ascent.

Resurgence: The point at which an underground stream emerges at the surface.

Samsara: The cycle of birth and death as described in the Buddhist religion.

Selenite: A crystalline form of Gypsum (Hydrated Calcium Sulphate)

Sink: The point at which a surface stream sinks below the surface.

Single Rope Technique (S.R.T.): The technique of descending and ascending a single rope to pass vertical sections of cave passage. In recent years, this technique has largely superceded the use of metal ladders for passing pitches.

Straw: A hollow, thinwalled stalactite that has the same diameter along its length, and looks like a straw.

Streamway: A cave passage occupied by flowing water.

Sump: A cave passage completely filled with water.

Siphon: The French word for a sump.

Tao: The *Tao* as described by Lao Tse is the cosmic process in which all things are involved—the ultimate, undefinable reality. Tao means 'Way,' or 'Path' in Chinese.

Traverse: Horizontal movement along a cave passage, some distance above the floor or along a wall or cliff face.

Tyrolienne: A horizontal rope tensioned between two belays that enables cavers to cross wide passages at height.

Wetsuit: A skintight suit of foamed neoprene rubber, which provides thermal insulation, but allows water in. Although the wearer is wet, he or she remains warm by virtue of the wetsuit effect.

0-595-22057-6

Printed in the United States
852200003B